Mixed Experiences

Mixed Experiences

Growing up mixed race –
mental health and well-being

Dinah Morley and Cathy Street

NCB's vision is a society in which all children and young people are valued and their rights are respected. By advancing the well-being of all children and young people across every aspect of their lives, NCB aims to:

- reduce inequalities in childhood
- ensure children and young people have a strong voice in all matters that affect their lives
- promote positive images of children and young people
- enhance the health and well-being of all children and young people
- encourage positive and supportive family, and other environments.

NCB has adopted and works within the UN Convention on the Rights of the Child.

Published by the National Children's Bureau

National Children's Bureau, 8 Wakley Street, London EC1V 7QE
Tel: 0207 843 6000
Website: www.ncb.org.uk
Registered charity number: 258825

NCB works in partnership with Children in Scotland (www.childreninscotland.org.uk) and Children in Wales (www.childreninwales.org.uk).

© National Children's Bureau 2014

ISBN: 978 1 909391 15 4
Ebook ISBN: 978 1 909391 16 1

British Library Cataloguing in Publication Data
A catalogue record for this book is available from the British Library

The views expressed in this book are those of the authors and not necessarily those of the National Children's Bureau.

Typeset by Saxon Graphics Ltd, Derby, UK

Contents

Foreword

Society appears to be changing at a fast pace, with services often trying to catch up. Attitudes towards children and young people, evidence about what makes them vulnerable, and ideas about how they can be protected and helped have all developed in a promising way in relation to even a decade ago. To some extent, so have perceptions of mental well-being and difficulties. Whether out of choice or necessity (probably both), the importance and weight of individual and collective cultural needs has become increasingly central across policy, the media, social sciences, public health and welfare sector planning and delivery.

These positives are often counterbalanced, however, by intolerance to diversity, particularly at times of economic crisis. Society often tries to encompass difference, only for progress to be clawed back for a variety of reasons, notwithstanding that population changes are of their own making. Just when we think we have grasped emerging trends and we attempt to apply them to front-line service thinking and models, we find ourselves, yet again, a generation or two behind. Dynamic constructs, like ethnicity, race and culture, drive change and are equally affected by it. Young people bring their additional dimensions, and these are only a part of their complex and interrelated identity needs, in a developmental journey that is far from simple. At the same time, making sense of their wholeness and uniqueness has probably become more challenging for adults. Children and young people of mixed or multiple race, heritage and other experiences particularly come to represent this rapidly changing world.

If we are to make sense of them, we need to take a number of fields and perspectives into consideration. The authors master this complexity wonderfully, by approaching mixed heritage young people from different angles, which they integrate throughout the book. Dinah and Cathy relate young people of today to sociological and developmental theories, research evidence, policies, changes in demographics, public attitudes and service patterns in order to conceptualise mechanisms that explain vulnerability and resilience, and that contrast the specific underpinnings of this young group to the general population.

What particularly brings young people to life are the extracts and quotes from a qualitative study with young adults of mixed heritage, who provide fascinating accounts of their experiences from childhood through to adulthood, and to becoming parents themselves.

Family, school and community roles are explored separately and in conjunction. Experiences of childhood, adolescence and peer pressure are contrasted with maturing grown-up views, adjustment and determination. It is interesting to hear study participants feeling 'pigeon-holed' by different single race groups, wishing to belong, reflecting on the role of physical appearance and self-esteem, explaining their perceptions of mental health, and finding it harder when they move from primary to secondary school. We share both turmoil and struggle ('I feel I belong nowhere, never been fully accepted') with resolution and the contentment of embracing several identities.

Dinah and Cathy offer no one-size-fits-all solutions, precisely because this is a heterogeneous and continuously evolving group of young people, as is our changing society. Rather, they successfully help the reader reflect at several levels, both overt and subtle, and to draw their own conclusions for practice with children and young people of multiple backgrounds.

Panos Vostanis
Professor of Child Psychiatry, University of Leicester

Acknowledgements

I would like to record my appreciation of Professor Susan Procter and Dr Paul Godin, at City University, who encouraged me through the research study. I was also generously supported by other colleagues in the research group.

I am indebted to People in Harmony, which helped me, together with Intermix and YoungMinds, to find people to talk to – both participants and people experienced in the field.

Many people have been generous with their time and interest, most of all the 21 participants who shared their stories and experiences so frankly and engagingly.

Lastly, my thanks to my collaborator, Dr Cathy Street, without whom my data might have remained in the university archives and without a future.

Dinah Morley

A number of people provided invaluable advice as the book form of Dinah's research emerged, and in particular I would like to thank Jo Tunnard and Judi Barker for their support and encouragement.

Both Dinah and I also appreciated the editorial advice and suggestions for how to focus what is a very complex topic, offered by Paula McMahon at the National Children's Bureau.

Cathy Street

Glossary

Throughout this book we are aware that we use terminology for race and mental health that can be controversial and about which people have differing and strong views. It is important to clarify our usage at the outset and our reasons for choosing these terminologies. The use of 'black' as a generic term is also considered.

Mixed race/mixedness

In the British vernacular the terms race, culture and ethnicity are frequently used interchangeably to describe the same phenomena in our 'multicultural society', referring to different countries of origin, shared religious practices and customs, epidermal difference and frequently class differences.

While accepting the fact that we are all one race and that genetically we differ very little from one another, between and across different groups, we use the term 'race' as it is commonly understood. The term 'mixed race' is employed throughout as being the term most used and preferred by those who were consulted to inform the 2001 UK Census (Aspinall and others 2006). It is interchangeable to an extent with the terms mixed heritage, multiple heritage, biracial, multiracial, mixed ethnicity and multi-ethnic.

Mental health

The term 'mental health' is specifically used to describe *health* as opposed to *illness*. Children's mental health has been variously described as:

- the strength and capacity of children's minds to grow and develop with confidence and enjoyment
- the capacity to learn from experience and to overcome difficulty and adversity
- the ability to live a full and creative life
- the flexibility to give and take in friendships and relationships.

Occasionally we use the term 'emotional well-being' in recognition of the fact that, for many people, 'mental' is often linked inextricably to psychopathology.

Mental health is something most people enjoy most of the time, but 10 per cent of under 16s at any one time have mental health disorders or illnesses, with this percentage likely to be considerably higher in the big conurbations (Office for National Statistics 2007).

Black

The term 'black' is sometimes used as a catch-all for non-white. The reader will be able to discern where this is the case in sections of the book that are direct quotes. Frequently in our society the term is used to differentiate from 'white' and, as such, includes Asian, Chinese and any others where there is an epidermal difference. As we will see, some participants in the research study have *passed* for white.

Introduction

Children and young people of mixed race experience difficulties in their childhood that are, or which they perceive as being, centred in their mixedness. These experiences are additional to the experiences of other children and young people. This book offers practitioners an insight into the experiences of racism, discrimination and identity confusion that children and young people encounter.

The data for this book are drawn from a qualitative narrative research project undertaken in 2007/08 (referred to in the book as the *Mixed Experiences* research). One of the key features of both the original study and this book is its reflective approach. Participants in the study were asked to reflect on their childhoods and their experiences related to growing up as mixed race children and young people. The study looked specifically at their emotional well-being, identifying risk and resilience factors that were present in their childhoods that might have impacted on their mental health and that they experienced and interpreted as being a consequence of their mixedness.

The data were collected around the time of Barack Obama's election to the US presidency in 2008 and some participants discussed the impact of his success as a mixed race man.

Introducing the *Mixed Experiences* study

Twenty-one participants (thirteen female and eight male) took part in the study; the characteristics of each participant, their ages, the countries they came from and how they were recruited to the study, are summarised in the Appendix to this book. Each is identified by a pseudonym, gender, age and the area in which they grew up.

The age range was 21–56 years, the majority being in their 20s and 30s, and overall, although the older participants describe significant difficulties associated with their mixedness, the young participants' accounts show many similarities.

The email narratives have been reproduced as they were written and the spoken narratives have been punctuated to retain as accurate a sense as possible of what was being conveyed.

A qualitative methodology was chosen in order to collect data that described intensely personal and very individual experiences. An interpretive phenomenological analysis (IPA) was followed in order to draw out the significant statements and to identify the themes that were important to the participants. A second-stage analysis focused on an understanding of how risk and resilience factors, as understood in the field of child and adolescent mental health (CAMH), might affect the experiences of mixed race children and young people.

Why this subject is important

Children and young people of mixed race are not an homogenous group. They may have very different experiences of childhood depending on where they have grown up, what they look like (that is, their skin colour) and the way in which their family, school and community supports their mixedness. The group's extreme heterogeneity does not allow for a one-size-fits-all assessment of their needs, and this is the challenge for practitioners.

Those working with children and young people of mixed race need to be aware of the particular risks to mental health/emotional well-being that may be present in the lives of these young people. This is not to pathologise mixed race, but rather to ensure that supports that are appropriate, relevant and robust are provided.

Proportionately, the mixed race group of children and young people makes up the fastest growing group of young people in England and Wales – a trend borne out by the 2011 Census data, which indicated that there are now around 603,398 children and young people of mixed race under the age of 18 in England and Wales population. On this basis, this population group is deserving of urgent consideration by practitioners in all services provided for children and young people.

Despite generally limited research, we know that mixed race/dual and multiple heritage children and young people are likely to have had a significantly different experience in some aspects of growing up when compared with their peers – both black and white. This can put them at greater risk of experiencing difficulties, but can also promote resilience in quite distinct ways.

For example, a number of research studies have pointed to the racism these children and young people suffer at the hands of both black and white peers; the difficulties they experience in seeking a safe identity; the negative school experiences; and the importance of family attitudes in ensuring that they become well-adjusted adults.

All of these often quite subtle and/or hidden experiences, and the tensions children and young people may face with both their families as well as the wider community in which they live, are issues that practitioners working with them, whether in health, social care, education or voluntary sector arenas, need to be aware of and consider in their everyday practice.

Issues raised by the study

The *Mixed Experiences* research highlights and develops our understanding of some of the complex experiences that children and young people of mixed race can face. These issues, explored later in this book, concern the following.

- The influence and attitudes of family members towards a child or young person's mixedness, the key role that can be played by mothers and the apparent denial of mixed heritage within some families, sometimes unintentionally, and sometimes reflecting a wish to protect the child or young person from possible repercussions of their mixedness.
- The considerable influence of school and the often unrealistic expectation, from both peers and teachers, that children and young people of mixed race will understand both sides of their cultural heritage.
- The range of complex factors that can result in a sense of isolation and identity confusion in these children and young people.
- The implications for mental well-being, including both the potential for greater resilience, but also the increased risks of mental health problems.

Intended audience

This book will be of value to all practitioners working with children and young people, especially those in the mental health field, and also in health more generally, early years services, social care, education, youth justice and the voluntary sector.

This is an area where not only is the current literature quite small-scale, but there has also been only limited analysis of the implications of being mixed race on a child or young person's mental health and emotional well-being. There are many studies, however, focusing on black and minority ethnic groups or on young refugees and asylum seekers (for example, Malek and Joughin 2004; Street and others 2005).

By exploring in depth the experiences of a small group of mixed race people reflecting back on their childhood experiences, and considering some of the key themes from other research studies, albeit a limited field, the *Mixed Experiences* research identifies the potential additional risks to mental health for the child or young person of mixed race and considers how resilience develops for some and not for others.

The book also discusses the policy context for promoting equality and challenging discrimination on the basis of race. It provides examples of projects or local services that have targeted mixed race children, young people and families, and points to the opportunities for learning from this small sector of provision that practitioners in other services might draw on to meet the needs of the growing population of mixed race young people.

Structure of this book

The book comprises nine chapters. Bearing in mind the time pressures of busy practitioners, these chapters have been kept as succinct as possible and, to a large extent, most can be read as standalone topics.

Chapters 1 to 4 are essentially background reading, setting out the national policy, legislative and political context. There is also a summary of current demographic data about mixed race children and young people. Chapter 3 provides an overview of the existing research on this topic and, in Chapter 4, the current thinking about the risk and resilience factors that can impact on children and young people's mental health is reviewed.

Chapters 5–8 explore in some depth the main themes arising from the *Mixed Experiences* research. These are the development of identity; growing up mixed race and family dynamics; school, community and inclusion; and geography and isolation. In Chapter 7 the implications of these findings in terms of what mixedness means for children and young people's mental health are considered, followed in Chapter 8 by descriptions of what is known about existing services for children and young people of mixed race. The final chapter then draws together the different themes emerging from the study and explores the implications for practitioners working with this often hidden group.

1 Setting the scene: The policy context

A number of factors within the policy arena can be seen as key influences on how children and young people of mixed race are viewed in society and, crucially, how certain areas of public policy have been developed with reference to individuals of mixed race.

A number of important historical influences, national policy and legislative measures that practitioners need to consider include:

- the debate about ethnic and cultural identity that came to prominence in the 1980s
- adoption and race
- equalities legislation and the public sector equality duty.

The identity debate

Mixed race issues were first debated in the UK in a significant way in the 1980s, often as part of the transracial adoption debate (Small 1988; Katz 1996). In these debates, there is a strong emphasis on the importance to mixed race children (usually at this time, white/African-Caribbeans) of needing to and being expected to identify themselves as black, acknowledging that many African-Caribbeans will have some racial mixing in their heritage. However, underlying this perception was a belief that being 'mixed' meant being 'mixed up' psychologically (Barn and Harman 2005) and an implicit belief that the adoption of a black identity would ameliorate this racial confusion. This notion of being 'mixed up' has been refuted in no small way by the obvious and public achievements of many people of mixed race, and there is a developing and popular view that racial and ethnic mixedness is a positive attribute (Nava 2007).

At the same time, the rising phenomenon of mixed race is sometimes presented as a product of the conditions of late modernity, a period exemplified by globalisation and characterised by de-traditionalisation, privativism and individualisation. These themes are central to works by writers such as Giddens (1991) and Beck (1992; 2008) when they examine the concepts of global and personal risk in the context of their writings on risk and late modernity.

Arguably, contemporary social conditions may provide a greater opportunity for mixed race people to forge personal identities beyond the traditional categories of class, race and nationality. However, work by Mahtani (2009) suggests that this 'freedom' was not felt by the participants in his study, and is challenged in the current discourse by a cautious approach to the idea that being mixed might be the future.

A more strident discourse has been gradually developing, spurred on by the controversial views expressed in the media during Barack Obama's campaign and election. From *The Guardian* newspaper to the *Evening Standard*, Obama's victory was hailed variously as 'A Great Week in Black History' and the arrival of the 'First Black President' in the United States. There followed a lengthy and often acrimonious development of the discourse, across the media, in which people of mixed race pointed out the fact that Obama was mixed race, as were other contemporary heroes such as Tiger Woods and Lewis Hamilton. This position was criticised by others, perhaps most stridently by Michael Paulin (2008), who declared: 'As a mixed race person, this racist attitude is something with which mixed race (people) are all too familiar. The implication is that we are only civilised because we have a white parent.'

Being different from the norm, in terms of needing additional or different supports, is a factor for many children and young people who are caught up in the health and social care services. For example, gender and ability issues are well established in professional practice as areas that require specific assessment and intervention strategies. Race is arguably more problematic in that it overlays other differences and, within a racialised society, adds a further complexity to the child's experience.

Although there are large numbers of policy documents focusing on race and equality aspects of assessment and service delivery, very little attention is currently paid to mixed race as a possible additional factor to be taken into account in assessment and intervention. Notwithstanding the fact that children of mixed race will in many cases have gender, ability and other differences, the possibility that their 'mixedness' creates an added dimension to their childhood experiences, which sits alongside any other specific differences, is deserving of further consideration.

The stories of the *Mixed Experiences* research participants, as they are quoted in the later chapters of this book, will provide the reader with some insights into these debates and it is hoped will inform professional practice and general understanding. As one of the participants in the study noted:

> *Don't bother about what people think of you, it's how you think inside. People will try to pigeon-hole you and some people might want you to choose. You may have to say you're black to fit in, and you might feel you don't fit in anywhere. But it doesn't matter what people think, in the end it's how you feel about yourself and it takes time to get to that point. You may not feel like that when you're younger but there will come a time when you're older you don't have to explain yourself to people. Just feel happy within your own skin that you're mixed race and that's something to be proud of. You can just say that you're*

mixed race and you don't have to put yourself in any other category. You are
mixed race and that can be the end of it really.

The adoption debate

The invisibility of mixed race children in practice and policy is also found in the longstanding debate on mixed race and adoption, influenced by Small (in Ahmed 1986; 1988) and Maxime (1986). In describing the motivations of adoptive parents, Small says: 'The concept of mixed race, which has become part of conventional social work language, is misleading because it caused confusion in the minds of transracial adopters. It can lead them to believe that such children are racially distinct from other blacks' (Small 1986 in Ahmed (ed) p. 91).

For many adoption services, 'black' has been the default racial grouping for children of mixed race, denying their white heritage regardless of their personal feelings about their identity, the way they are viewed by others or their early lived experience. Although eminent practitioners, such as Small, do not categorically say that black children should never be adopted by white parents, there is still, in 2013, a perception that local authorities do not make 'transracial' adoption placements.

The position of the mixed race child is not specifically addressed in these debates, although the importance that has historically been attributed to race as an overriding criterion for allocating adoptive parents is evident in the ministerial foreword to the latest *Adoption Guidance* (Department for Education 2011):

> *I want to move away from the situation where children are kept in care for a long time simply to find a family of the same ethnicity when a suitable family of a different ethnic background is available who can meet their other needs. To say the obvious, parents from one particular background can be loving, sensitive and successful adoptive parents for children from very different backgrounds and that must be our primary consideration. Local authorities must consider all of the child's needs and not place the issue of ethnicity above everything else, though this must be taken into account. I know that children tend to do well when placed with a family who shares their ethnic or cultural background, but I know also that delay can have a very detrimental effect. It reduces the child's chances of finding a family and has negative consequences on their future development. If there can be an ethnic match that's an advantage, possibly a very significant one. But, it should never be a 'deal-breaker'.*

While this calls for a more liberal approach to racial and ethnic matching in the adoption system, tacitly acknowledging the priority given to race as a criterion for allocating adoptive parents, the guidance makes no reference to children of mixed race who are over-represented in public care and in the health and welfare systems generally.

Few of the people in the *Mixed Experiences* research study had any direct experience of the welfare system. Where lives had been particularly difficult and children and young people had been received into care, experiences were not positive, as they are not for many. However, while the reasons for poor care will be specific to the particular circumstances, the child of mixed race is likely to interpret this as being because of her or his mixedness.

The comments made by many in the *Mixed Experiences* study underline the need for children and young people of mixed race to have their heritage properly recognised, supported and valued. Failure of service providers to understand this is highly likely to mean that the services they provide for children and young people of mixed race, when they are not optimal, will be regarded with suspicion, and prejudice will be suspected.

Equalities legislation

The Equality Act 2010 is an important influence on all health and social policy relating to children, young people and their families. The 2010 Act came into effect in October of that year and replaced previous legislation such as the Race Relations Act 1976, the Sex Discrimination Act 1975, the Disability Discrimination Act 1995, the Equality Act 2006 (Part 2) and the Equalities Act (Sexual Orientation) Regulations 2007. In April 2011 a public sector equality duty (Section 149 of the Equality Act 2010) also came into force, which applies to public bodies and requires them to consider how different people will be affected by their activities; its aim is to support robust decision-making to ensure that efficient and effective services are accessible to all, and that they are able to meet different people's needs.

Although the Equality Act 2010 does not make specific reference to mixed race people, this legislation is recognised to have strengthened the law in various ways in order to tackle discrimination and inequality on the basis of 'protected characteristics', one of which is race and which includes ethnic or national origins, colour and nationality.

Various reports have explored the possible implications of the Equality Act 2010 in terms of health and social care, and also what the Act means for schools. For example, the NHS employers' briefing (NHS Confederation 2010) highlights the fact that the Act refines various concepts and definitions, including that it is unlawful to discriminate against someone because others think that they have a particular protected characteristic, even if the person does not actually possess that characteristic – so called 'perception discrimination'.

With regard to schools and the implications of equality legislation on how they work with and support children and young people, *Research Report 70: The Equality Duties and Schools*, produced by the Equality and Human Rights Commission in 2011 (Bukowski and others 2011) notes that this is an under-researched area within education. The research that has been done suggests fairly patchy progress, and the authors note (in the Executive Summary, page v) that certainly up until very recently, 'only a minority of schools had action plans for racial equality that were clearly linked to targets and actions in school development plans'.

In response to this lack of research, the Equality and Human Rights Commission employed Ipsos MORI to undertake a detailed programme of research to examine how schools in England and Wales were implementing equality duties and to identify examples of positive practice. Ipsos MORI was also asked to gather data about awareness of the then forthcoming public sector equality duty and to draw lessons from how schools have implemented equality duties, which might inform guidance and the successful implementation of the public sector equality duty.

Ninety per cent of the schools contacted by Ipsos MORI reported actions or activities that they had implemented in order to meet the race equality duty, with positive practice including work to raise awareness, tolerance and understanding; the holding of multicultural days and assemblies; forging links with schools and communities overseas; using interpreters; building links with parents; and dealing with racist incidents.

The report also notes (Executive Summary, page x): 'The most commonly cited positive impact is an increase in pupils feeling valued. Schools also mention improved attainment at key stages and in subjects; better engagement and higher aspirations; narrowed gaps in performance; increased wellbeing, and reduction in racist incidents.'

Crucially, however, the research found that the majority of the schools contacted (62 per cent) were unaware of the forthcoming public sector equality duty. Schools identified the main barriers to fulfilling equality duties as a lack of time and money; a lack of guidance; a lack of relevant training; confusing legislation; and the need to convince parents or carers to take equality duties on board.

Conclusions drawn by the Commission were that the majority of schools was engaged with the importance of equality and that there were clear signs that the duties were having some impact on their actions and pupil outcomes. While this is good news, the downside is that there is considerable variation in the types of equality-related actions and activities overall and, to quote the authors (Bukowski and others 2011, Executive Summary, page xv), there is a need for: 'Greater emphasis on action-planning and using evidence. Schools have good intentions and policies or schemes, but would benefit from translating these into more actions that can be measured.'

Cultural competency

All of the policy initiatives noted so far in this chapter apply to all children and young people. Equally, the 11 standards of the *National Service Framework for Children, Young People and Maternity Services* (Department of Health 2004a)

– both those that are universal and those that are targeted – relate directly or indirectly to the delivery and/or preservation of good mental health. The standards cover health promotion, disability, safeguarding, the management of medicines and the provision of services for children who are hospitalised, as well as mental health specifically.

What is important to bear in mind, however, is that while physical disability and geographical location are identified as service access issues, racial or ethnic difference is not identified as a primary difference. This may be intentional in the overarching documents, because further detail is given in guidance documentation, and it is also expanded upon in a separate document concerning Standard 9 – *The Mental Health and Psychological Well-being of Children and Young People* (Department of Health 2004b) – where there is acknowledgement (at page 8) that services for children and young people, 'should be provided irrespective of their gender, race, religion, ability, culture or sexuality … to ensure greater equity is achieved'. It is further noted (at page 13) that the 'mental health needs of minority communities are currently not being specifically met by mainstream services', and that 'services need to be sensitive to these differences and ensure that staff are equipped with the knowledge to work effectively with the different groups represented within the community they serve'.

In a subsequent report detailing progress in the implementation of Standard 9 of the *National Service Framework* (Department of Health 2004c) in a section entitled 'Delivering Race Equality', similar points about the need for culturally sensitive services are made, and it is noted that, although there are examples of good practice, there is still 'some distance to go' before all groups in the community have their needs met. This report notes that commissioners and providers must ensure that they are meeting their statutory duties under the Race Relations (Amendment) Act 2000, specifically in relation to promoting equality of opportunity and eliminating discrimination; they should be using the government programme, Delivering Race Equality in Mental Health Care, to inform their strategic planning and commissioning of services, which should be underpinned by three 'building blocks':

- appropriate and responsive services
- engaged communities
- better information.

The report also sets out as a 'marker of good practice' that the needs of specific black and minority ethnic groups within each community are represented in local child and adolescent mental health services (CAMHS) needs assessments, stating (at page 47):

> *The concept of cultural sensitivity applies to the whole community. In order to deliver services that recognise the needs of both the majority and minorities in the population, clinicians have to be trained from the outset to consider the question of how to deliver services in a culturally appropriate way, at all times.*

What is key, however, in thinking about children and young people of mixed race, is that while inclusion is central to the development of the subsequent discussion and guidance, and attention has been paid to the needs of black and minority ethnic (BME) children and young people, those of mixed race have generally been included within the BME category and have been identified by their non-white ethnicity.

This is also evident in the work of the National CAMHS Support Service (NCSS), which came to an end in March 2011. The NCSS, with its many partners, including non-statutory organisations, developed guidance and tools for the assessment of BME children and young people, enabling CAMHS to become culturally competent. However, this work did not have a particular focus on children and young people of mixed race. Even within the range of material available for BME children and young people, issues that might be important for those of mixed race are rarely identified and much less explored as integral to their assessment, other than by the small number of projects set up specifically for this group.

Similarly, in an earlier, adult-focused document entitled *Inside Outside: Improving Mental Health Services for Black and Minority Ethnic Communities in England* (National Institute for Mental Health in England 2003), people of mixed race are not identified separately. This is the case in many local policy documents across the UK and, although patients/service users are encouraged to identify their racial mix, rather than just ticking 'other', requirement to consider the specific needs of children and young people of mixed race is hard to find.

The key factor in raising awareness of the existence of people of mixed race was the expansion of ethnic categorisation in the 2001 UK Census, which allowed for people of mixed race to specify their parental mix for the first time, and many public data sets are subsequently using these new categories. This provides scope for an examination of the demographics and the socio-economic experiences of people of mixed race, but there are considerable limitations to this data that must be borne in mind.

International influences

In the last few years, issues of mixed race have been more prominent in the national discourse as a result of Barack Obama's victory in the 2008 US presidential election. Obama is the son of a white American woman and a black Kenyan man who met at the University of Hawaii and, without any doubt, his election has lifted the hopes and aspirations of black and non-white people across the globe.

One of the study participants, Emile, a young man living in Belgium with a white mother and a father from Mauritius, shows both his own vulnerability as a mixed race person and the profound effect Obama's election had on him in the following extract from his story. Emile says:

Obama made me realize again that you can overcome anything no matter who you are or where you're from or whatever people think you to be. He is mixed. The most powerful man in charge on the planet (arguably) is mixed, is a person of color ... represents everyone all over the world who felt bad for being who he/she was, he gives hope ... he gives me hope ... I know he's 'just' a man and idolizing someone can be a dangerous thing ... but, what he has done makes me feel like being a part of something.

This statement is a striking illustration of the sense of 'not belonging' that many children and young people of mixed race experience, frequently being seen by their peers as 'too black to be white and too white to be black' – something Obama himself commented on in a speech given in Philadelphia on 18 March 2008, where he noted that some political commentators had deemed him 'too black' whereas others saw him as 'not black enough'. A consequence of this for many children and young people may be a struggle, especially in their teenage years, to settle on an identity that fully values their racial heritage and provides a comfortable place to be.

Summary

This brief overview of some of the policy issues and influences that are relevant to children and young people of mixed race illustrates the many complex factors that may impact not only on their personal development, but also on the public services that they may use. Contradictory and often negative stereotypical views, issues to do with globalisation and large-scale changes to the make-up of populations, and more recently, new legislative imperatives, all combine to present practitioners with a challenging picture of understanding how to work sensitively and effectively with this population group.

What complicates matters still further – a factor mentioned at several points in this chapter and a prominent theme in the review of literature and research summarised later in the book – is that while there are large numbers of policy documents and research studies that have focused on race, as yet very little attention has been paid to individuals of mixed race. The urgent need to rectify this gap is evidenced in the next chapter, in which what is known in terms of demographic data and national statistics about mixed race children and young people is summarised and discussed.

2 Mixed race young people: A growing sector of society

In order to provide a context for the reader, a digest of available statistical data, showing the relative position of young people of mixed race across a range of social indicators, is presented in this chapter.

Key points to note include:

- Despite limitations and gaps in the data, based on UK Census figures, the numbers of children and young people of mixed race make up a growing proportion of UK society. Furthermore, their numbers are growing disproportionately faster than any other section of the child population.
- Given the heterogeneity of people of mixed race, and the fact that there have only relatively recently been opportunities for them to register their mixedness, or for their mixedness to be registered, such data may give a partial or inaccurate picture. Social influences also play a role in how individuals identify themselves.
- There are very few data sets that effectively identify a mixed race category. However, from the limited data that exist, there are concerns about the over-representation of children and young people of mixed race in relation to some issues of social concern.

Changing UK demographics

In the 2001 UK census 666,034 people in England and Wales (1.2 per cent of the total E&W population) were identified as being of mixed race, of whom 360,355 were under 18. Figures from the Office for National Statistics (ONS) show that by 2009 this figure had risen significantly to 986,600. In the latest census in 2011, the figure had reached 1,224,400 (2.2 per cent of the E&W population) of whom 603,398 were under 18.

While there are still difficulties in establishing accurate figures with regard to the numbers of mixed race people within the UK population overall, the ONS data clearly indicate that the known numbers of mixed race children and young people are increasing significantly.

What available statistics tell us

Data that show trends – for example, demonstrating demographic changes and identifying areas of inequality – are useful as checking mechanisms. Such information has the potential to alert practitioners to variables and issues that they may hitherto have neglected, as may be the case in relation to the care and support for mixed race children and young people. It is in this context, while acknowledging their limitations, that the following data are presented.

There are very few data sets that effectively identify a mixed race category. Many research projects have a 'black' classification and an 'other' into which people of mixed race might place themselves. It is also equally possible that people of mixed race will identify themselves as white. For example, information based on the 1991 Census exemplifies the social construction of such data. When the results of that Census were analysed, 230,000 people had written mixed heritage on the form in the 'other black' or 'other ethnic' category.

Following further research, it was clear that people were becoming more keen to identify as 'mixed' and wanted to be able to accurately record their mix (Bradford 2006). We can only speculate about the reasons for this, but the growth in numbers of people of mixed race, the political agenda around equalities in the 1980s – such as the work in schools undertaken by the Inner London Education Authority (ILEA) – and the increasing presence in the media of people of mixed race, are highly likely to have influenced these choices about self-identity.

Using longitudinal data, Bradford (2006) revealed that 15 per cent of mixed race people who were classified as white/black Caribbean in 2001 had opted for 'black Caribbean' in 1991 and that 29 per cent had identified themselves as 'white'. This could be a reflection of the way in which the entries were analysed – for example, someone electing to be identified as 'mixed white' would have been counted as 'white' – but it may be indicative of how some people of mixed race see themselves in terms of what they experience as their predominant culture. Another possibility is that the information could have been provided by the white parent, as the head of household, and this may have been a factor in influencing this categorisation.

Despite the limitations and gaps in data, it is evident that the number of children and young people of mixed race has almost doubled over the 10 years from 2001 to 2011. However, the proportion of people in the different mixed race groupings varies considerably, underlining the fact that this is by no means a homogenous group.

Concerns about over-representation

Although a wider reading of the statistical material suggests that people of mixed race are not over-represented in many areas of social concern, there are some significant exceptions in a number of important domains. Owen and Statham (2009), looking at disproportionality in child welfare generally, note that children of mixed race are: 'over-represented in every category – being high for children in need (5.0 per cent) and more than double their population percentage (3.5 per cent) amongst children on the child protection register (7.4 per cent) and amongst those looked after (7.8 per cent)'.

The Department for Education and Skills (2006a) identifies 8 per cent of children in care as being mixed race, although they made up only 3 per cent of all children.

In London, BME children and young people have been identified as using the child and adolescent mental health services (CAMHS) disproportionately more (Audit Commission 1999: 15), this reflecting the larger numbers of BME families choosing to live in the London area. Although these data do not identify individuals of mixed race, a disproportionate number of mixed race children and young people are seen in in-patient CAMHS (Tulloch and others 2007). Furthermore, BME young people are disproportionately represented in the numbers of young people detained on adult wards: in a study by the Mental Health Act Commission (MHAC) in 2004, 26.8 per cent of young people detained on adult wards were from ethnic minorities, and while Black African and Caribbean communities make up only 2.9 per cent of the youth population, they accounted for 13.1 per cent of the young people detained on adult wards (Department of Health 2004b).

The age and location profile of the mixed race population affects the interpretation of other data. For example, mixed race young people are proportionately more likely to be in higher education, proportionately more likely to be involved in drug offences and to be victims of crime, being younger and living predominantly in the large conurbations. However, while the young mixed race population taken as a whole is more likely to live in London, white/Asian and white/Caribbean young people are less likely to do so (Bradford 2006). Although the data are complex, young people of mixed race also appear to be more harshly treated in the youth justice system (Feilzer and Hood 2004).

While mixed race young people are doing less well overall in terms of GCSE passes, there is again considerable variation within the mixed race category, with white/black Caribbean young people performing worst and at the same level as the black Caribbean group, which performs worst of all (Department for Education and Skills 2004). These outcomes are more closely linked to poverty, as measured by free school meal eligibility, than race (Tikly and others 2004).

In relation to early pregnancy, white/black Caribbean young women have some of the highest rates, but there are similarly high rates in the white community and black Caribbean community (Department for Education and Skills 2006b).

In terms of data about disadvantage, an unclear picture is presented about the position of mixed race children and young people. While we must question the wisdom of looking at data on mixed race as if they present a homogenous category, the dramatic growth of this 'mixed' child and young person population, and its disproportionate representation in some areas of disadvantage, demands exploration and attention in terms of a more refined understanding and appropriately sensitive service provision.

Possible implications for mental health and emotional well-being

As we will see in the next chapter, very little research exists that specifically examines the general well-being of mixed race children and young people, and even less addresses their mental health/psychological well-being and the implications for professional practice. This is particularly significant in assessments for mental health/psychological well-being, for social care, and for the ways in which children and young people of mixed race are supported in school.

Despite the extensive epidemiological and clinical research that has been conducted into the mental health needs of all children and adolescents generally stretching back over more than half a century, and the growing awareness of the impact of disadvantage on children and young people (Hirsch 2007), very little of this research has focused specifically on the needs of children from BME communities. Even less has focused on mixed race children, who have rarely been identified as a group for any service focus, or investigated as a separate group to inform service development.

Summary

The recording of mixed race children in health, social and educational statistical reports, although increasing, is still extremely patchy, with almost no longitudinal studies in which they are reliably identified as a separate group, thereby greatly limiting the gathering of any data on trends. Most usually they have been assigned to the 'other' category. Large quantitative studies, from which the risk and resilience factors for mental health and emotional well-being are derived, are therefore unlikely to have gathered any reliable evidence on the specific issues that are important to mixed race young people and that might be affecting their mental health development or other aspects of their lives.

This gap in our knowledge requires attention given the striking demographic trends described at the start of the chapter. Furthermore, given the well-documented difficulties of access to mental health services experienced by BME children and young people (Malek and Joughin 2004, Malek 2011), we need to ask whether there is a need for health, social care, education and youth services to do more to ensure equality and appropriateness of access and support for children and young people of mixed race. At the very least, it seems reasonable that services work to ensure that this is on a par with what is now provided for other groups.

3 Influences on the mental health and emotional well-being of mixed race people: Themes from the research literature

This chapter focuses mainly on UK material but also includes other references, in particular from the US. It is important to acknowledge that the UK experience of racism has a different historical trajectory from that of the United States, where the 'one drop rule' is still a strong influence and as a result the construction of mixedness is somewhat different.[1] Overall, much of what is written on mental health and mixed race is dispersed within studies of mental health in relation to race/ethnicity and studies of mixed race people more generally.

Studies of identity development specifically are not included here because much of literature covered has ample contextual material included within it that deals with identity, drawing for example on the work of Root in the US, and Barn and others in the UK (for example, Tizard and Phoenix 2002; Katz 1996).

Key points to note include:

- Mixed race children and young people can experience what has been termed 'cultural homelessness' when experiencing the tensions that can develop when loyalty to their parents' cultural and racial identity conflicts with a need to be accepted by the outside world, and in particular, their peer groups.
- Other research, however, suggests a much more positive outcome for some children and young people of mixed race, and argues that identifying themselves positively multiracially, rather than identifying with only one side of their ethnic heritage, leads to more positive psychological outcomes.

---

1 An historical colloquial term in the United States for the social classification as black of individuals with any African ancestry; meaning any person with 'one drop of black blood' was considered black.

- Research focused on experiences in schools indicates that children and young people can be affected by seeming 'invisible'; they can experience racism from teachers and from black and white pupils.
- In some research, racism has been identified as a significant risk factor for children and young people developing self-destructive behaviours.

Mixed race children and young people and mental health

Much of the research and auto/biographical literature on mixed race inevitably covers issues that impact on mental health/emotional well-being, focusing as these studies do on family relationships and the racism of the outside world. Many references are made to the traumatic experience of secondary school, to the difficulties of establishing an identity, to strategies for dealing with racism – all factors that have the potential to affect mental health adversely.

The following four contributions from the US are included because they specifically illuminate issues of risk and resilience.

Elaine Pinderhughes (1995), in her discussion of the relative merits of mixedness, identifies two barriers to the achievement of a healthy identity for mixed race children, setting out the positive and negative contexts for these children that are relevant across national boundaries.

- The continuing denigration in our society of the minority group to which they are connected.
- The non-existence of a multicultural ethnic group to which they can feel connected, causing the invisibility of biracial existence.

She goes on to describe the primary factors in producing a positive growing-up experience for interracial children as:

- geographic location, where the sense of difference is minimised
- the degree and quality of parental understanding and help with racial issues.
- support from the wider family and community
- acceptance of both parts of their racial heritage, which can be done by maintaining positive connections with individuals from both ethnic groups.

Pinderhughes draws attention to the dynamic properties of racial identity and the tensions that can develop when loyalty to parents conflicts with a need to be accepted by the outside world, a position that is described in a paper by Vivero and Jenkins (1999) as 'cultural homelessness'. This wide-ranging paper explores the possibility that the mixed race child will become hyper-vigilant to cultural clues, asking questions at an early age about where he or she fits in, and having to learn different cultural meanings for different situations.

Vivero and Jenkins suggest that there may be a developmental disruption to learning, which may be internalised by the individual as failure and inadequacy. However, these authors (at page 21) acknowledge that 'multicultural people' may have some advantages from being in a 'culturally enriched environment but that where the demands of their close relationships exceed the child's developmental capacity, there may also be problems'.

They go on to say (at page 21) that this 'extensive repertoire' that the mixed race child acquires may stimulate cognitive strengths: 'but at the cost of confusion and errors when cues are ambiguous or the demands exceed developmental resources'. The paper describes the treatment approaches for those individuals who are suffering from 'cultural homelessness' and promotes the use of this term as helpful in allowing the patient to see that she or he is not 'crazy'.

While this paper appears to subscribe to the view that mixed race means mixed up, the authors do point to the strengths and potential resiliences of mixedness. This complexity is mirrored in some autobiographical writings, which deal with the complicated and often difficult journey through childhood, but culminate in strong and resilient adulthood.

Ten years later, Binning and others (2009) continue this theme in a paper that specifically looks at psychological well-being and mixedness. Based on completed questionnaires from 182 young mixed race people at high school, asking them which groups they identified with among other questions on self-esteem, the results show (page 35) that 'those who identified with multiple groups tended to report either equal or higher psychological well-being and social engagement'.

Binning and others (2009) conclude that identifying positively multiracially, rather than identifying with only one side of your ethnic heritage, leads to more positive psychological outcomes. They suggest that 'embracing multiple group memberships' means that people have decided to voice their multiracial status rather than subsume it into one group, with all the consequences of that suppression. This leads them to conclude that there is something 'unique' about these individuals and their resilience.

The risk and resilience theme is explored in a more recent study of American Indian youth (Mmari and others 2010). Although this is not a study of mixed race, it is of interest in that it identifies the factors that increase risk and protection/resilience and particularly cites racism as a significant risk factor that motivated the young people in the study to violence and self-destructive behaviours. Racism was less of an issue where the community was more isolated from the mainstream, but it was strongly experienced in school where there was a lack of teacher support and strong peer pressure to not do well academically.

Mental health and ethnicity

There is an extensive literature examining the historical and current relationship between race and mental illness, largely focusing on the abuse of power relationships considered by a number of writers to be evidenced by the disproportionate numbers of black adults detained in mental hospitals (Fernando 2003). Much of this literature applies to all ages and as such it is not specific to children and young people.

The work by Littlewood and Lipsedge (1982) is one of the earliest and best known of such writings in the UK. In particular, their work drew attention to the disproportionate numbers of black people who are in receipt of compulsory in-patient care, diagnosed as schizophrenic. The authors offered a number of possible reasons for this. They described the 'Afro-Britain' as being in a double bind position in society, suffering from the deprivations of poverty as well as racism, but suggested that this is not the whole story.

Fernando (2003) argues that it is the inherent racism in the health system that causes a disproportionate diagnosis of psychosis to be made in black people, and catalogues the apparent reluctance of health professionals and others involved in health systems to challenge this. His views are strongly held by many in the field.

A further strand in the literature looks at the psychological health consequences of the stress caused by racism itself. Williams and others (2003), in their review of the relevant research in the US, point out (at page 206) that:

> ... the subjective experience of racial bias may be a neglected determinant of health and a contributor to racial disparities in health. Perceptions of discrimination appear to induce physiological and psychological arousal, and, as is the case with other psychosocial stressors, systematic exposure to experiences of discrimination may have long-term consequences for health.

More recently, there has been a greater focus on these issues and further refinement of the debate. The *Aetiology and Ethnicity in Schizophrenia and Other Psychoses* (AESOP) study (Morgan and others 2006), a robust multi-centre research programme, finds higher rates of first episode psychosis in black people than in the general population in the UK, although it does not find that this is the case in the Caribbean. In common with Littlewood and Lipsedge, though 24 years later, the AESOP team also suggests that socio-economic factors must be playing a part in this finding, concluding that the differences revealed are a product of the social disadvantage experienced by black people and migrants generally.

Bhui (2002) had already raised the potential psychological damage that misidentification could inflict in his discussion of the psychosocial and psycho-political aspects of racism. He concludes (on page 44): 'Misidentification, to be considered not to be who one believes one is, to be denied preferred identities that are precious, are akin to psychological mutilation or annihilation. Identity is cherished, even at the expense of it being illusory and temporary.'

The debate about the relative effects of these factors is ongoing and demonstrates that mental health services need to adapt and change to allow BME populations to access help in a more timely and culturally appropriate way. The virtual absence of mixed race people from this discourse is noteworthy, although the above quote from Bhui has enhanced meaning for people of mixed race. The politics of health in relation to ethnicity and culture are complex. These are reviewed by Hillier and Kelleher (1996), stressing the need for an awareness of cultural practices and beliefs whilst not 'pathologising' culture; an issue fully explored in the same book by Ahmad (1996).

Kramer and Hodes (2003), who provide a good overview of the mental health of African-Caribbean children, point to a number of biases that could be operating to distort the picture in relation to children of mixed race. They cite the inherent racism of those making the diagnosis as well as a range of socio-economic and developmental factors. They refer to a study by Goodman and Richards (1995) that found that BME young people were over-represented in the diagnosis of psychotic disorders, mirroring the research findings in relation to the adult population. They go on to say, citing Tizard and Phoenix (2002), that many young people of mixed race identify themselves as black, which is also likely to confuse the results of any surveys.

Mixed race children and young people and emotional well-being

The following UK texts discuss the emotional well-being of mixed race children and young people, and represent current thinking generally on mixed race issues. No one study looks exclusively at risk and resilience in relation to mental health but the data collected across these studies provide compelling evidence of both.

Ilan Katz (1996) undertook a small study from a psycho-dynamic perspective to research the development of identity in the mixed race child. His study shows that children of mixed race do not necessarily identify with the black community and are influenced by their childhood environment and the links that are made with the black/non-white family. This work moves on the debate of the 1980s about the proper care of children of mixed race/mixed parentage, which focused to a significant extent on the development of the black identity of these children (Maxime 1986).

Katz describes the families that he interviewed as being in 'a constant process of negotiating difference' and points to the hostility experienced from both black and white extended families. He identifies class as a fundamental factor in all his participant families and concludes (Katz 1996: 174) that: 'class affected the family life style more than race and culture'.

A major piece of UK research that looked at the circumstances of mixed race children is that of Tizard and Phoenix (2002). Based on earlier work undertaken in 1993, their study looked at the racialised identities of mixed race young people and analysed a sample of 58 young people aged 15–16 in 32 different schools. They found (page 115):

> *a not very strong relationship between having a positive identity and attending a multi-racial school, and a much stronger one between currently wishing they were another colour, and the strength of their affiliation to white people. Because siblings differed in their racialised identities, we suspect, also, that family dynamics and the self-esteem of the young people are influences on whether their racialised identity is positive. Having a positive racialised identity was not associated with living with a black parent.*

This study, which draws attention to the importance of family and self-esteem as well as differing sibling identities in the experience of the child of mixed race, demonstrates the importance of not jumping to conclusions and recognising the heterogeneity of the mixed race population.

Parker and Song (2001) draw together much of the thinking on mixedness. A contribution to their book by Ifekwunigwe describes a research project in which she interviewed 25 mixed race people and selected six of these to listen to in depth. The stories of three women are reproduced in her chapter. The women look back at their childhoods and describe many of the situations identified by participants in the *Mixed Experiences* research, such as the prejudices of both black and white people towards them, the extreme difficulties of secondary schooling and the coming to an appreciation of their mixedness in young adulthood.

These same issues are described by Alibhai-Brown (2001), who provides a personal account as well as a comprehensive digest of the discourse of mixedness. She interviews a random selection of people of mixed race and, within this, clear class differences emerge. She provides evidence of identity dilemmas and the same sense of 'sitting on the fence' that is regularly referred to in the discourse of mixedness. She also finds families where there is a sense of loss of one identity and where children will be encouraged to marry back into the lost identity to redress the balance. 'I sometimes think I betrayed my people' (by marrying a white woman) says one of her interviewees (at page 81). Others prefer to identify as black although they have one white parent, and others who 'pass' for white describe the uncomfortable place this can be.

The contextual material in Olumide's (2002) work traces the history of race and mixed race and provides a comprehensive overview of current discourses. The research element of the work is based on 35 interviews and two workshops with a roughly equal number of men and women of mixed race, with a range of ages and class backgrounds. Although her participants describe many difficulties, there is a strong emphasis on the positive features of mixedness – for example, the ability to span two or more cultures and to understand and experience the differences at first hand. However, these are outweighed by the negative impact of external forces and, whilst accepting that her sample is not wholly representative, she concludes (at page 118):

'they [her participants' views] do serve to suggest that much energy is expended on considering responses to definitions imposed from "outside"… The mixed race condition is constructed as a problematic state.'

Mixedness in school

Ali (2003) looks at the lives of mixed race children in three primary schools. She spends time with them in school and at home, describing the situational differences that were evident in the way children related to her in different environments. Her study also graphically shows that children are preoccupied with very different concerns from race and colour, although they struggle to deal with their mixed parentage, helped to some extent by the presence of mixed race people in the media. Ali points to the differences in the schools that she visited, in terms of location and intake as well as ethos, and the impact of that on how racism and racist behaviours happened and were perceived. She does not find that the schools are dealing appropriately with multicultural issues, although teachers on the whole recognise the importance of these. She sums up (at page 265):

> The failing school policy in the area of multiculturalism in the schools visited is only one such area of concern. I believe that this research has implications for family studies, 'race', ethnicity and cultural studies, as well as ongoing concerns within feminism about the continued hegemony of the acquisition of normative gendered positions.

A study undertaken in London by Barrett and others (2006) is based on interviews with 12 British Bangladeshi and 12 black-white mixed heritage young people, as well as a quantitative questionnaire with 569 pupils from three inner London schools. The research endorses Ali's finding of the importance of location. In this inner London setting the authors found there was no feeling of marginality or being between two cultures, rather that identities were 'fluid and contextually contingent'.

Tickly and others (2004) point to the fact that mixed race pupils experience racism not only from teachers but also from both black and white pupils. Teachers interviewed in their sample explained the difficulties of their mixed race pupils as being because of identity issues, and teachers were convinced, incorrectly, that the majority of their mixed race pupils lived in single white parent families, with mothers who could not deal with racist abuse. They demonstrate how this racism links with peer pressures to precipitate mixed race boys particularly into a downward spiral of poor achievement and 'unacceptable' behaviour.

They go on to describe the 'invisibility' of mixed race pupils in school and the need for all young people to be seen more holistically in terms of their identities. They highlight the lack of a common terminology to describe pupils of mixed race, both in schools and in policies, as a possible restricting factor in terms of schools being able to identify and respond to the needs of their mixed race pupils.

They conclude that the barriers to achievement of white/black Caribbean pupils are the same as those for black Caribbean pupils – for example, social disadvantage, institutionalised racism (in terms of low teacher expectation) and exclusion from school. However, the researchers are careful to point to the heterogeneity of the mixed race pupils, whilst flagging up the consistent underachievement of white/black Caribbean boys within the mixed race group.

The data collected by Tikly and colleagues suggest that there may be a need to focus supportive measures on specific groups of young people of mixed race. They report that social disadvantage, as evidenced by the free school meal eligibility rate, is shown to be closely linked to the relative levels of achievement in that the proportion of white/black Caribbean pupils on free school meals (33 per cent) is around twice the national average (16 per cent), with the level for white/black African pupils (28 per cent) also being high. For white/Asian pupils the proportion is closer to the national average (19 per cent), suggesting that this higher achieving group is financially generally better off.

Educational practice in relation to mixedness is discussed by Williams (2011), who bases much of her book on work done by the Multiple Heritage Project (now known as Mix-d: and described in Chapter 8). She provides insights into the lives of the pupils who attend the groups and conferences, and includes useful teaching resources. She calls for more opportunities in schools for mixed race pupils to discuss issues of identity and emphasises the need for a whole school approach.

Parenting mixed race children

The research by Caballero and others (2008) assesses the perspective of the parents of mixed race children. The study participants are 'ordinary' mixed families and the researchers seek to understand the day to day parenting of mixed race children from the parental perspective. They focus on how parents give their children a sense of belonging and heritage, negotiations around these areas, and the opportunities and constraints. A questionnaire was distributed through schools in England and Wales to find parents of mixed families. An interesting finding from the 35 subsequent interviews is that 'mixed parenting is not just about mixedness'. While the parents in this study had a variety of concerns in dealing with mixedness, the researchers point out (at page 28) that these 'pale into insignificance when compared with the other considerations they face in their everyday parenting'.

Their concerns were those of any parent for the safety and security of their children, again a caution for making any sweeping generalisations about the mixed race group. The findings also show that the mother is the main caregiver and disseminator of custom and practice in the family, having 'on the whole' more time with the children, as in most families generally.

The Caballero and others' (2008) research emphasises the heterogeneity of the mixed population and the variety of ways in which families deal with mixedness to support, ignore or emphasise it. The authors find that the main difficulty anticipated by the families about their children's mixedness is the reaction they will get from the outside world, and they call for changes in social policy and practice to better reflect this heterogeneity.

Okitikpi (2009) picks up this theme from a different perspective in his study of inter-racial relationships of 20 African and African-Caribbean men and 20 white women. He finds that these relationships are subject to intense scrutiny from wider family and beyond, unlike mono-racial intimate relationships. In some cases hostility is intense and partners go through personal crises, a process described by Aymer (2010) and evident in many autobiographical accounts. Although these crises are dealt with subjectively, there is a commonality of experience. Once again it is the interaction with the outside (racist) world that creates the tensions for inter-racial partnerships, which inevitably affects the children of those partnerships.

Adoption and family experiences

There is a significant literature that explores transracial adoption placements of BME and mixed race children – for example, the writings of Small and Maxime in the 1980s and Park and Green (2000). Patel (2009) is one of many writers on this topic and she describes the experiences, gathered between 2000 and 2003, of adoptees aged 21 to 43, showing how they constructed their identity as they grew up in white families to achieve a fully transracial identity.

There is growing interest in the experiences of mixed race children who grow up in single parent families. Harman (2010) looks specifically at the position of lone white mothers as they manage the upbringing of their mixed race children in the absence of the black parent. Her work is based on interviews undertaken in 2004/05. Harman is interested in the changing nature of white privilege that these mothers experience as they confront the prejudices of the outside world when they are seen with their children. The extent to which the presence of a black father in the family, although intimately related to class, appears to offer an altered dynamic to the experience of mixedness was touched on in the work of Tizard and Phoenix (2002) and deserves further exploration by academics in this field.

Younge (2010) deserves a mention in this review. His book (*Who Are We – and Should it Matter in the 21st Century?*) provides a wide-ranging picture of race, sameness and difference. Younge describes the gamut of mixed existences from the intermarriage of Tutsis and Hutus, through the 'one drop' rule and its contortions, to those of apartheid, through the 'cablinasianism'[2] of Tiger Woods to a new social identity of mixedness as this is developing

---

2   A portmanteau word used by Tiger Woods to describe his ethnic make up. *Ca* for Caucasian, *bl* for black, *in* for American Indian and *asian* for Asian (namely Thai) (Allwords.com).

in the West. Younge's work underpins the socially constructed nature of race and the economic forces that have been, and are still, dependent on racial categorisation. Although the human race comes out badly in terms of prejudice and compassion, the book perhaps heralds a more thoughtful future.

Summary

The writings included in this chapter have been selected to provide a context for practice and to demonstrate that there is a need for an in-depth understanding of the mental health of mixed race children and young people.

From this brief overview of the main, relevant literature strands it is evident that there are additional potential risks to the mental health of children of mixed race. Okitikpi (2005) makes a significant contribution to practice issues, covering mental health issues while looking at identity development. There are full references in the work to many aspects of working with mixed race children and on intermarriage, its history and the perceptions around the children of mixed marriages. Williams (2011) also provides practical support for teachers in ways to support pupils of mixed race, based on her experience with the Multiple Heritage Project.

In summary, a very heterogeneous picture emerges, with family and location being important influencers of the developing identity and self-esteem of young people of mixed race. While the racism in the external environment is perceived as challenging and essentially the root of conflict, mixed race children also struggle with many of the same issues as mono-racial children as they grow up and establish themselves as adults. However, throughout this literature there is evidence that not belonging to either the black or the white group is a significant stressor, particularly in the teenage years.

The stories from the *Mixed Experiences* project build upon and develop this literature further. They demonstrate the extent to which class, poverty, geographical location and race are intertwined, something that the historical perspectives and the epidemiological studies in the literature consistently show. Mixed race people are seen differently in different contexts as Theo, one of the study participants who grew up in the Cayman Islands with an English father and a Jamaican mother, explains: 'Well the white crowd (at university in the UK) assumed I was black, as well actually, so I was like apparently I'm black. I don't really care. But you know whereas in the Caribbean you are probably pushed more to the white side when you're mixed race.'

4 Risk and resilience relating to mental health

Nationally, and increasingly in the past two decades, there has been a greater recognition of the central importance of mental health to all aspects of child and adolescent development, both from government and from experts in the field. This chapter examines the concepts of risk and resilience as they are used in the field of child and adolescent mental health (CAMH), as likely indicators of need and possible emotional difficulties.

An understanding of risk and resilience, as these terms are used in CAMH, is widely acknowledged to be of value for every practitioner working with children and young people, not least those who may be facing challenging life circumstances.

Key points to note include:

- The likelihood of these risks being prevalent in the lives of children and young people of mixed race needs to be thought about by practitioners during assessments of need.
- Development of resilience is important and can happen as a result of being well supported through difficult times; a supportive family and a positive school environment are key factors in managing risk and developing resilience.
- Many children and young people are on a continuum of risk and resilience, emerging as confident adults in most cases.

Later in the book the issues of risk and resilience are considered specifically in relation to the data gathered through *Mixed Experiences*. What follows here is a summary of the concepts of risk and resilience as they relate to *all* children and young people.

What do we mean by risk and resilience?

There is a general acceptance among practitioners working in health and social care that the co-existence of a number of adverse social, health and economic factors can put children and young people at risk of mental ill-health. On the other hand, so called 'protective' factors – situations, circumstances and relationships that bolster and protect mental health – exist for most children and young people, which help them to develop resilience to cope with difficult situations.

This process of the development of resilience, which takes place as children meet difficult situations in life and are supported to get through them, is sometimes described as the 'steeling' or 'inoculation' effect, operating in a similar way to a physical inoculation against disease. Factors such as nurturing schools and supportive families promote resilience, but the absence of these positive features in the child's life if he or she experiences, for example, the death of a close relative, can have the reverse effect (Rutter 2007).

The Health Advisory Service (1995) report describes risks to child mental health in relation to the three domains – the child, the family and the environment. These 'risks', when they are present in sufficient number and/ or severity for the individual child or young person, severely compromise their chances of good mental health and put them at risk of mental disorder. Table 4.1 summarises these.

Table 4.1: Risk factors for the development of mental health difficulties in children and young people

Type of risk	Risk factors
Risks in the child	– Genetic influences – Low IQ and learning disability – Specific development delay – Communication difficulties – Difficult temperament – Physical illness, especially if chronic and/or neurological – Academic failure – Low self-esteem (a factor in almost all of the above but can occur in a seemingly unrelated way)
Risks in the family	– Overt parental conflict – Family breakdown – Inconsistent or unclear discipline and lack of boundaries – Hostile and rejecting relationships – Failure to adapt to a child's changing developmental need – Abuse – physical, sexual and/or emotional – Parental psychiatric illness – Parental criminality, alcoholism and personality disorder – Death and loss
Risks in the environment	– Socio-economic disadvantage/poverty – Homelessness – Separation or displacement from the family – possibly as a result of disasters relating to acts of God or acts of war – Discrimination and exclusion – Other significant life events such as moving house, changing schools, parent remarrying, parental redundancy or sudden illness

In Table 4.2, Wallace and others (1997) summarise the different risks factors in the child, the family and in the environment. These have been identified through analyses of research and clinical observations of children and young people, as well as by gathering information from parents, teachers and social workers. Drawing these data together, Wallace and colleagues have tabulated the indicative rate of mental disorder in children against these risks.

Table 4.2: Prevalence of specific child and adolescent mental health risk factors and impact on rate of mental disorder (Wallace and others 1997)

Risk factors	Impact on rate of disorder
Risks in the child **Physical illness**	
– Chronic health problems	3 times increase in rate overall
– Brain damage	4 to 8 times increase in rate of disorder in youngsters with cerebral palsy, epilepsy or other disorder above the brainstem
Sensory impairments	
– Hearing impairment (4 per 1,000)	2.5 to 3 times more disorder
– Visual impairment (0.6 per 1,000)	No figures but rate of disorder thought to be raised
Learning difficulties	2 to 3 times increase in rate, higher in severe than in moderate learning difficulties
Language and related problems (2%, but better methods of identifying required)	4 times rate of disorder
Risks in the family	
Family breakdown (divorce affects 1 in 4 children under 16 years of age) Severe marital discord	Associated with a significant increase in disorders (e.g. depression and anxiety)
Family size	Large family size associated with increased rate of conduct disorder and delinquency in boys
Parental mental illness	
– Schizophrenia	8 to 10 times rate of schizophrenia
– Maternal psychiatric disorder	1.2 to 4 times the rate of disorder
Parental criminality	2 to 3 times rate of delinquency
Physical and emotional abuse (of those on child protection registers, 1 in 4 suffer physical abuse and 1 in 8 neglect)	Twice rate of disorder if physically abused and 3 times the rate if neglected
Sexual abuse (6.62% in girls and 3.31% in boys)	Twice rate of disorder if sexually abused
Risks in the environment	
Socio-economic circumstances	Gap in applicable evidence base
Unemployment	Gap in applicable evidence base
Housing and homelessness	Gap in applicable evidence base
School environment	9% in grades 1 to 9 are victims of bullying 7 to 8% of children have self-reported bullying other children themselves
Life events	
Traumatic events	3 to 5 times rate of disorder; rises with recurrent adversities

Understanding of risk and resilience

Awareness of the fact that children and young people could indeed have mental health problems grew largely out of the experiences of those who were evacuated or orphaned during World War II. In 1952 the World Health Organisation published a work by John Bowlby called *Maternal Care and Mental Health*. It focused on what was known about maternal deprivation as it appeared to relate to the emotional capacities of the child to make subsequent meaningful relationships with others. The report studied the needs of children who were orphaned and/or separated from their families, particularly focusing on their mental health.

A year later Bowlby published his seminal work, *Child Care and the Growth of Love* (Bowlby 1953), which is based on the earlier report and in which he draws attention to the use of physiological measurements, suggesting that electro-encephalographic studies would be of interest, effectively pre-figuring the recent important work on the development of the infant brain.

Over the past two decades there has been an increasing recognition in national policy terms of the importance of an understanding of risk in relation to child and adolescent mental health and the central importance of the very earliest childhood experiences in establishing patterns of brain activity that govern subsequent behaviours.

Supporting vulnerable families is an accepted tenet of health and social work practice and is also recognised as important in the school and justice environments. The risks for mental health where parenting is not 'good enough' and where attachment is fractured or non-existent, and the consequent need to develop children and young people's resiliences are now understood by most practitioners.

This understanding underpins many of the large scale government initiatives of the last decade, including the *Every Child Matters* programme (Department for Education and Skills 2004), which set out five key outcomes for children that practitioners are expected to have in mind when assessing and planning for children generally, and children in need specifically – namely, that children are healthy; stay safe; enjoy and achieve; make a positive contribution; and achieve economic well-being.

The importance of early support to families is embedded in the standards for mental/emotional well-being that were set out in a sister document, the *National Service Framework for Children, Young People and Maternity Services* (Department of Health 2004a), where there is an emphasis on the provision of high quality, child-centred and personalised care. These themes continue in the more recently published *No Health Without Mental Health* (Department of Health 2011), which outlines the UK coalition government's policy and sets out the standards for mental health services across all age groups.

Supporting children and young people to develop resilience

Most children and young people will experience one or more risks to their mental health when growing up. Generally they manage to cope with these through a combination of the possession of a secure personal identity and being in receipt of secure, solid support – usually from family – which develops and sustains their resilience.

The Health Advisory Service (1995) report, citing Rutter (1990; 1989), identifies the three key domains of resilience as:

- self-esteem, sociability and autonomy
- family compassion, warmth and absence of parental discord
- social support systems that encourage personal effort and coping.

Many children and young people suffer from low self-esteem, shyness and not being very sure of themselves, but as adolescents and young adults they emerge as confident people. This continuum from risk to resilience begins in infancy and develops, often unevenly, as people mature into adulthood and benefit from new, affirming relationships and achievements.

Rutter (2007), considering the life span theme, stresses that good interpersonal relationships are significantly associated with resilience, and that (page 206) 'this applied to relationships across the entire life period from childhood to middle age'. These suggested ingredients of resilience, particularly those relationships within the family, together with the apparent inoculation effect of the successful management of early adversity, are evidenced convincingly by the stories of the participants in the *Mixed Experiences* study.

As a result of the increasing understanding of resilience and its importance for mental health, many schemes have been developed to support children and develop resilience. Some of these are projects in local authority children's centres and some are in schools. For example, the Nurture Group movement, which flourished in the 1970s and 1980s, provided vulnerable young children with a nurturing school environment to help them to flourish against the odds of their 'risky' circumstances.

Since that time, large-scale initiatives such as Sure Start and in-school schemes such as Place2B and Pyramid, Circle Time and a number of anti-bullying programmes, all work to promote individual resilience. Specific schemes that focus on the needs of BME pupils are also following this approach, largely through supporting academic achievement and raising aspirations. The education and poverty programme run by the Joseph Rowntree Foundation throughout the past decade is a notable example here (Kintrea and others 2011).

While most of these programmes evaluate well in the short term, it will be some time before the long-term benefits can be fully identified and quantified.

Research about risk and resilience and mixed race children and young people

Currently there is a paucity of research and little is known about any additional risk factors that might have an important part to play in the assessment of need in children and young people of mixed race. From the *Mixed Experiences* research study it is evident that there are significant factors, over and above those that may be experienced by many children and young people, and therefore the potential for the consequences of these factors, if not ameliorated, to precipitate emotional difficulties that may endure into adult life. Thomas, one of the participants in *Mixed Experiences*, with an English mother and a Jamaican father, reflected on this:

> *Perhaps I've experienced so much alienation of the imperceptible kind (uncertain of whether others' unspoken hostility or my misreading of their silence has left me out in the cold) that separating myself forcibly from the group would be one intolerable step further. Of course, that may plainly be a human trait: people of all ages have an undeniable need to herd themselves. But I've lived my life so far with the belief that the majority is confidently carousing its way through the world while I'm somehow behind glass, unable to cross the threshold.*

The data from *Mixed Experiences* have been interrogated to identify factors that might promote or impede the mental health/emotional well-being of mixed race children and young people, through the exploration of risk and resilience factors that might be exclusive to the experiences of this group. These are discussed later in the book as the experiences reported by the study participants are explored.

These experiences make it clear that there have been significant risk factors for mental health in their growing up, as can exist for any child. How far these relate to being mixed race can only be inferred from the words of the participants themselves and are closely interwoven with family, class and economic status. It is important too, to separate the proximal and distal factors in these experiences – that is, those factors that directly impinge on the individual's day-to-day life and those that may be causing or affecting the direct experiences. For example, some interesting questions arise as to whether the proximal experiences emanating from parental relationship breakdown are, or are not, caused by the more distal effects of the parents' mixed relationship.

Summary

This chapter has briefly outlined our knowledge and understanding of the risks to children and young people's mental health, how resilience can be promoted and the importance of building resilience in children whose lives are particularly challenging. Some of the early influences on our understanding have been summarised. What is evident, however, is that although inclusion and the development of services that are culturally competent are prominent themes, the focus has been largely on BME communities. Little attention has been paid specifically to the potential needs of children and young people of mixed race.

In the following three chapters, the findings from the *Mixed Experiences* research are presented. These reveal a complex picture of the lived experience of growing up as a mixed race young person – some positive, but others much less so. Collectively, they highlight the importance of refocusing our thinking in order to ensure that the needs of mixed race children and young people are given the attention they warrant.

5 Growing up as a mixed race person

The participants in the *Mixed Experiences* study raised a wide range of issues that have obvious relevance to their emotional development and subsequent well-being as adults. In this chapter, the following issues are considered:

- how their appearance affected the development of their identities
- the importance of families and
- the influences of attitudes of family members.

In Chapter 6 some of the wider influences external to the family are described – namely, participant experiences of isolation and marginalisation and the often significant influence exerted by school and local communities.

Key points to note include:

- Many of the study participants show that they were confused about their identities at the adolescent stage and had strong feelings about their appearances during particular periods of their growing up.
- Skin colour is important in how young people of mixed race are seen and categorised, and can sometimes deflect from true identity. Many young people of mixed race go through times when reality and self-concept conflict, and are in denial of their mixed origins. Although identities are becoming more fluid in today's Britain, young people of mixed race are still likely to find themselves outside the group.
- Parents, in particular strong mothers and grandmothers, are shown in the study as important in helping children to develop resilience; furthermore, families who are affirming of their child's mixedness help to develop resilient young people.
- Perceived, though unintentional, family denial of a child's mixed heritage can often reflect a wish to protect the child or young person.

The development of identity and appearance

For most of the participants, the data show that during early childhood racial/ethnic identity was not particularly significant and generally friends paid scant attention to racial difference. But, emerging from childhood, young people find themselves abruptly in a different world. The adolescent phase is one in which peer group relationships are cemented and when identity as part of a peer group is important.

For many young people this is a fraught process in that it coincides with entry into secondary education, requiring both a physical and emotional transition as well as a time when peer group pressures exert themselves and relationships with peers assume an equal or greater importance than family relationships. The data indicate that children of mixed race often find themselves outside the group, excluded by others who were good friends at an earlier developmental stage. This echoes the findings of a number of research projects focusing on children of mixed race (Tizard and Phoenix 2002; Ali 2003).

Kathleen, one of the *Mixed Experiences* participants now in her 40s, describes how she experienced being different in her primary school but shows that it was not significant to her at the time in the way that it later became:

> I didn't really understand that I was different until I was about 5, when I went to school. My parents tried to explain to me about my colour when I asked why I was brown, in simple language that a child can understand, something to do with mixing white paint with brown paint and that the result was me, you know that kind of thing, and I was happy. Life was very simple until I was about 11 when I went to secondary school then it all changed!

Staged theories of identity, such as Erikson's, describe this adolescent phase as a period when young people are 'remarkably clannish' and 'cruel in their exclusion of all those who are "different", in skin colour or cultural backgrounds' (Erikson 1977: p. 236). Erikson suggests that this is in itself a defence against identity confusion.

Group identity and the existence of the 'in-grouper' and the 'out-grouper' (Tajfel and Turner 1986) are exemplified strongly in the *Mixed Experiences* data, showing that children of mixed race who cannot find a group to belong to are always in the position of the out-grouper.

Being able to identify with a group enhances self-esteem and, in the post-Erikson era, identity is seen as shifting and changing to meet external demands or perceived demands. Thus the individual can swap identities to fit in more closely with the peer group by becoming an in-grouper on a temporary and utilitarian basis. Many of today's young people move fluently from group to group, modifying language and behaviours from classroom to peer group and from home to other social settings. For children of mixed race, who are struggling to find their primary identity, it is likely that managing these identity modifications will be a more difficult task.

Emile, who described his alienation from black and white groups at different times, attempts a resolution through a strong musical allegiance: 'I had severe identity crisis, didn't know who I was and where I could fit in. I found refuge in hip hop music. It spoke to me on a whole other level and gave me the feeling of being understood.'

Mixedness and self-concept: 'Do people see me as I am?'

Racial and cultural biases are developed as individuals compare their race/ethnicity with their own self-concept. This is likely to be another difficult area for the mixed race young person whose self-concept may not accord with that of the group to which she or he aspires. Those participants who 'passed' for white throughout their childhood were accorded in-group status with their white friends and were obliged to subscribe to the higher status accorded to this grouping. At the same time it is clear that they felt uncomfortable with this position.

Several participants talk about not looking sufficiently mixed, and, as a result, feeling compromised in the company of white friends because of being able to 'pass' as white. It is clear that white friends, although evidently not overtly racist, made some racist assumptions as Carla illustrates: 'I sit with white people and talk about things and talk about issues and I think they're talking to me as a white person, some of the things they say if they knew I was mixed race they wouldn't say things like that really.'

An enjoyment of 'difference', which embraces feelings of 'otherness' in the majority of participants, is an interesting and optimistic finding. Rob describes the contrast of this position with how he had felt growing up: 'I used to think that this meant I was neither white, nor black, but I have come to realise that *I am both*. Perceiving myself as being neither was debilitating. *Realising* I'm both is more positive and much more empowering.'

However, it was not a universal finding and two participants certainly felt strongly protective of their children, or future children, in wanting those children to be clearly established as black. This is a shift from the high status seeming to attach to 'whiteness' that is exemplified by other participants. Kathleen describes her difficulties with boys as a young person, and her position as an adult:

> Today being mixed race is 'fashionable' and all the young black guys want to date mixed race girls. When boys entered my life it was even more confusing. If I dated a white boy, the black girls who had hated me previously, suddenly thought I was betraying my 'race' and if I dated a black boy, my white friends were terrified of him!

These data demonstrate that the participants were significantly preoccupied with establishing their racial/ethnic identities as children and young people. It is also evident that over the period of childhood and into adolescence and young adulthood, ideas and feelings about identity change dramatically, from not being very aware of difference in early childhood to acute awareness and wanting to belong in adolescence, to wanting to be seen as who they are and the mix that they are as young adults. While Kathleen accepts that being mixed race is 'fashionable' in current times (a point made by several participants), she has been so affected by her own negative experiences as a mixed race child that she has been determined to avoid this experience for her own children, to the extent of restricting her choice of marriage partner to a black man.

She emphatically says that she wouldn't have children with a white man and yet she herself is half white and could perhaps have just as reasonably elected only to marry a white man. Kathleen was very influenced by her black grandmother as a small child but felt that her own mother favoured her sister who looks white, illustrating the complex interplay of ethnic and family influences.

Kathleen describes her skin colour as brown and says that her best friend, who was black, jettisoned her because she was too white. As an adult she has effectively elected to be black, challenging race/ethnic theories of high status/low status in so doing. As Tina says, commenting on Obama being described as the first 'black' US president: '… black of course is a far more safe place to be' – the assumption being that it is better to be identified as black rather than mixed.

Appearance: 'Do people recognise my true heritage by my looks/skin colour?'

Physical appearance has had a profound effect on the identity development of many of the research participants. The information they shared contains many references to how others saw them, as people of mixed race, as well as references to how the participants experienced their own physical appearances as children. The apparent need for both black and white people to pigeon-hole or categorise people of mixed race was raised frequently.

As we have seen, several participants 'passed' for white as children, being able to do so because they looked white to outsiders. To themselves they had features that came from their black/non-white heritage and they spoke of resentment that others defined them as white and did not recognise their true heritage.

A number of participants describe being seen as southern European rather than as mixed race or black. Sarah, whose father is Guyanian, enjoys this experience: 'I like people not knowing – I've had all sorts, am I Spanish, am I Iraqi and Iranian, am I south American? I quite like it, I think it's quite funny.'

However, others find it demeaning and an uncomfortable place to be and are keen to establish their own particular mix. Participants who describe their skin colour as dark or brown often struggled to have their mixedness recognised. Ayesha, whose father is Pakistani, describes her attempts to explain her mixedness and a friend's rejection of her Englishness/whiteness:

On numerous occasions I would try to fend off hostile approaches and questioning by saying that my mother was English, but this was to little or no avail, as I realised that it was my appearance that caused the most aggravation.

One friend actually advised me not to mention my dual heritage as 'you don't look English'.

The data provide numerous references to the difficulties of explaining mixedness and in getting true racial heritage properly recognised. Skin colour is a powerful factor in this experience, effectively categorising people as either 'white' or southern European, and, depending on context, black. Unsurprisingly for people growing up as mixed race in the UK there was a greater incidence of being described by others as southern European. It is impossible not to conclude that racism was playing a significant part in these categorisations – a reflection of the higher status accorded by Western society generally to fair skinned people.

However, the data also show that skin colour is registered differently in different settings, as is evident in Jack's experience as a Creole being brought up as black, and in Theo's experience in the Cayman Islands as well as in the US and in the UK, where he was seen as more white in Jamaica, more black in the UK and mixed (the norm) at home in the Cayman Islands.

The negativity with which some participants saw their own physical appearance as children gives more cause for concern. Some participants describe a real hatred of their 'dark' appearance, including a dislike of their hair and complexion. In the main this happens with adolescence when identification with the in-groupers becomes important, as does appearance more generally. Louise describes very strong negative feelings as a teenager, which still persist and cause her distress:

I felt really disgusting when I was that age – I felt really dark and aware of my looks. I had this really big thing about hair and darkness and yuk – shave it, pluck it, everything – it plagued my life and it still does now. I had laser treatment this morning – and I can't afford it and I do it and ... I really hate this in myself but I have to accept it and you know wish I could deal with it – but I was very unhappy about my features, my darkness.

Louise grew up in a 'white' environment and feels that her difficulties in developing sexual relationships as a young adult had 'something to do with the darkness'.

The experiences the participants described are concerning. From very different life situations, a number felt negative about their blackness. The internalised self-concepts of these people, who as children and young people of mixed race have encountered and had to deal with racism expressed in the most intimate ways, can only be guessed at. This negativity is highly likely to have implications for their future emotional resilience.

The importance of families

The importance of a strong and supportive family is universally recognised. In the previous chapter, the issues of risk factors and the development of resilience were presented, both of which have clear connections to family experience. While these apply to all children and young people, there are some factors that potentially apply very specifically to children of mixed race – namely, the possible risk of family relationships being hostile and rejecting of the mixed relationship and subsequently the children from that mixed relationship.

In the *Mixed Experiences* study, a vast amount of information was provided from the narratives about how participants' own families reacted to their mixedness. For example, the mixed marriage of their parents; their parents' capacities, or lack of them, to understand their mixedness issues; and the support they received from parents in dealing with problems that they saw as being related to their mixedness.

Strong black mothers and strong white mothers emerge from the narrative whose attitudes help to develop resilience in their children. Carla gained valuable insights into her mixedness from talking with her mother and sharing her experiences:

> *My mother's always been very pro black … she's always said I'm a black woman … she's always been like that quite militant in a way. I've grown up knowing about her experiences and her experiences of racism and knowing that it's difficult and knowing about the challenges and stuff like that so I can't be a white person. I've got more of an understanding of it and in a way I know about racism and I know about things like that.*

However, there is other evidence that suggests that in other families the issue of mixedness was denied or at best superficially dealt with. Some of the participants described a lack of family understanding of these issues, with others alluding to this denial as one of their parents' ways of trying to protect them – one commented that 'they probably thought that if you don't speak of something it ceases' while another suggested that his parents largely avoided discussion because they 'wanted me to grow up as a normal kid'.

This suggests that much of the denial is deeply invested in the aspirations for their children and in the protection of the children from the repercussions of their mixedness. Mary, for example, reports a lack of connectedness to her parent, saying she never really had a conversation with her mother about her mixedness, other than to be told to ignore racist remarks.

These findings from *Mixed Experiences* echo other studies. The apparent denial of the mixed heritage of their children may not have been the intention of the parents. White parents, particularly lone mothers like Thomas's, are frequently subjected to racist remarks and more extreme racism (Harman 2010). Parents' behaviour may derive from a genuine lack of ability to deal with the situation, resulting in denial of reality to protect both themselves and the child. Banks (2002) says that white mothers are often in denial of the 'observable reality' of their child's mixedness, and are unaware of, and incapable of doing anything about, the unmet identity needs of the child.

Possibly as a result of this denial, several participants grew up knowing little or nothing of their racially mixed heritage. Tracey, who knew little of her

Chinese family, describes seeing her grandfather on his deathbed when she was 10 years old and that she 'didn't view him as anybody really related to me'. Mary also suffered confusion arising from a lack of knowledge about a parent's ethnicity. She noted:

> As a mixed race person growing up I felt very confused because my mum didn't really have a conversation about my colour, it was almost like it had been swept under the carpet and wasn't really talked about. I wasn't really around my Iranian culture and I know even at my age now I feel a real sense of loss.

Carla, Kathleen, Sarah and Louise, however, describe their families as very affirmative of their mixedness. Sarah explicitly feels her family was seeking to develop in her pride about who she is:

> … my wider family as well, but definitely my mum and my dad, always brought me and my brothers up to be very proud of who we were. They were always saying that it's good to be different it's good – you know you should be proud of the fact that you can say that you come from nearly every continent in the world. We were very much brought up to not even think of it as unusual and whenever incidents would come up my parents would be … they would just sort of remind us that we're perfectly normal, there's nothing wrong.

In some instances the response from the family to mixedness is evidently influenced by educational standard and class, but this is not always the case. The stability of the family appears to be the significant factor and taken together with class and education, in some but not all cases, provides a background where a strong sense of pride can be instilled in the young person and where an ability to withstand and/or ignore racist insults and actions can be developed.

Access to wider family and visits to parents' home countries

For some participants the wider family – that is the family other than birth and/or immediate parents – has had a significant presence in their lives. Overall, the mothers' parents are shown to be more in touch and more influential in the family network, illustrating the importance of the mother's line as the dominant cultural transmitter. However, the data show that many factors affect this, including geographical location of some parts of the wider family, as well as the dominant cultural influence in the home. There is some indication that where the mother's influence is dominant there is frequent contact with maternal relatives, but again there is no clear pattern. Dominance of fathers' influence is not shown to relate to access to paternal relatives consistently either.

Strong, influential white and black grandparents also emerge, supportive of their grandchildren's mixed heritage, though differing in their ways of doing this. Kathleen, who purposefully elected to have a black partner as an adult, was very close to her black grandmother. Her Jamaican paternal grandparents lived with her family until she was 18. Her grandmother had a key role in her daily life, caring for her after school and listening to her daily experiences. She describes her grandmother movingly:

> *She told me family stories etc. of when she was growing up – she was the family philosopher. She had very little formal education, but she loved books! She learned through me too – my opportunities became hers if you know what I mean! She rejoiced in my achievements in the way that grannies do. Although not mixed race herself she had seen the way that mixed race people were treated in her lifetime, and she said to me when I was older (about 18 just before she passed) that every child is a precious gift from God, and that to receive the gift that is given but not look after and cherish it, is a sin against the God that gave it to you.*

This account exemplifies the importance of strong attachment to the caregiver and security within the family generally. Kathleen describes a grandmother who held her in mind constantly and loved her unconditionally, substantially taking on the mothering role, and who espoused a deeply held Christian philosophy.

The *Mixed Experiences* data present a complex fusion of culture, geography, wider family attitudes and of the personality/resilience of the parents themselves, as can be seen in Tracey's account:

> *… because of my mom's marriage "into whiteness", that whole side of my family was very distant from me. I never knew my maternal grandmother, and my maternal grandfather spoke no English and had had a stroke by the time I was born, so the few times I met him I never talked to him. He had been very opposed to my mother's marrying a white man …*

As a result of this discord, some of Tracey's Chinese relatives who lived close by were rarely visited. In contrast there was a much closer relationship with her father's family, although they lived in different cities. Tracey provides a number of examples of her father's apparent desire to distance himself from her mother's culture. This is possibly the most graphic:

> *… my father always expressed his dismay at going to (banquets held in a restaurant in Chinatown), at the 'dirtiness' of the restaurant or the strangeness of the food. One time he went so far as to take my brother and cousin, who were both young boys at the time, around the corner to McDonald's for dinner, so repulsed he was by the lack of cleanliness of the dishes. What kind of message did this send to us?*

In the gendered nature of parenting, Tracey's story is unusual. As has been noted above, mothers are generally seen as the most significant influence on the child's experience, passing on their culture and being the educators of their children. However what seems to be more important in terms of Tracey's family's identity is the place of her growing up – that is in the US – where the influence of her father and his culture was predominant.

Other participants in *Mixed Experiences* described positive experiences of having close contact with family on both sides, seeing them frequently. Other experiences of visiting relatives who were living in very different circumstances were alienating. Louise, for example, describes the visits to her Jamaican birth father as:

... looking in on the kind of like black kids in the community and visiting my dad at the weekend and kind of hearing the lingo and kind of I could pick it up a bit with my large Jamaican family – British Jamaican family – but always feeling slightly jealous, slightly resentful, slightly bullied, slightly outcast from that kind of connection, that kind of scene the black scene, what ever it is.

Louise, like others in the study, has a desire to immerse herself in the 'black' side of her family, but has found cultural expectations hard to manage. Other participants, Ayesha and Mary, had virtually no contact at all with one side of their families, although enjoying strong bonds with the other side. As young adults, they have both tried to remedy this situation without very much success and some disappointment, with Ayesha describing her upbringing as: 'almost totally bereft of any knowledge of my father's Asian heritage and language because he chose to ignore it completely'.

Their story is rather different from those of Tracey and Theo who went to the country of their other parent for their education, as well as the experience of the culture and possible family contact.

These two quite different accounts of attempts to re-engage with the lost or unknown family suggest a desperate need to know and be accepted by the absent parent, in common with many young people who are not mixed race who have been deserted by one parent. For the mixed race young person this search takes on an extra dimension of cultural difference and confusion.

The inferences that can be drawn from the data, on this hugely varied experience of inter-generational and wider family contact, alert the practitioner again to the extreme heterogeneity of experience influencing the lives of mixed race children and young people and therefore the dangers of making any prior assumptions.

Sibling differences

A striking finding from the narratives has been the existence of differences between siblings in the ways in which they have created their identities. Sometimes this has been as a result of siblings being brought up in different areas for substantial periods of their childhood, but more interestingly it is also related to skin colour as Carla describes:

... my sister isn't very much of a mixed race and I've had these kind of discussions with her about it before. I don't know what she classes herself as really but she ... kind of thinks if you don't look mixed race then obviously you're not mixed race ... I've got another sister – she probably sees herself being more with white people – she looks even more white than I do. In my family my cousins are mixed race and all of us are different. We go from looking white to looking mixed race and we all have the same sort of mix.

Tracey was close to her darker skinned sister but their blood relationship was sometimes not recognised by others because of their differing skin colours and Ayesha's experience shows how complex this can be when she describes all her brothers and sisters having appearances that were slightly different to hers.

Anna's account of her brother, and the way his chosen identity has informed his choice of marriage partner and the development of his persona, shows that he has established an identity that is radically different from hers – a process that has driven them apart:

> My brother who is now married he's assimilated into the community and to all intents and purposes he's written off his Asian identity – the woman he's with is a racist as far as I'm concerned ... The other thing she's done is persuaded him to change his name so he no longer has two Asian names he's got two English. I now have to call him P (English name) – his name's M (Asian name). He really wants to be seen as just another English man – whereas I'm the totally ... I love the fact that I have this unusual background.

Overall, the data suggest two broad types of sibling relationship. One is characterised by close sibling relationships, with siblings not necessarily looking very alike but sharing a common understanding of their mixedness. A second group seem to identify through skin colour, selecting their friendship groups accordingly and growing apart from siblings who look different. Although not all the participants would divide in this way, the stories show an unconscious (and sometimes very conscious) epidermal prejudice being played out in these familial settings.

Summary

This chapter has presented some of the key themes from the *Mixed Experiences* data concerning the participants' perceptions of the influences affecting the development of their identity, in particular the role of immediate family members but also more distant relatives. It is evident that physical appearance, and physical differences, are complex influences on these relationships, not least in terms of the sibling relationships just described. Intergenerational aspirations or, alternatively, disappointment, can sometimes lead to discontinuities and tensions that children and young people then have to negotiate their pathway through. For the practitioner, this again emphasises the need to understand and fully appreciate the diversity of experience of mixed race children and young people.

6 Wider influences of school and the local community

After the family, the school shows itself to be the greatest influence on childhood development and the establishment of personal autonomy. The experiences described in this chapter vary considerably, from very positive to very negative. Most participants experienced secondary school as tough and employed a variety of tactics to survive. The difference between primary and secondary school experiences mirrors findings of Ali (2003) and Tizard and Phoenix (2002), which show that other factors than race tend to preoccupy children at the primary school age.

Key points to note include:

- The influence of school on children and young people of mixed race is considerable. Its impact may be felt in two quite different and distinct ways – instilling in the child or young person a determination to succeed or resulting in a wish to leave education as soon as possible.
- There is often an unrealistic expectation, from both peers and teachers, that children and young people of mixed race will understand both sides of their cultural heritage. Frequently 'mixed' was equated with 'black'.
- Children and young people of mixed race value multicultural environments such as those found in London and other major conurbations, but this does not mean that there is an absence of racism, or that this can prevent feelings of isolation and social exclusion.

Surviving school

The participants described a variety of tactics for getting through school days, which, for a significant number, were experienced as being excluding and demoralising. For some the process built their resilience and determination to succeed, others just wanted to get out as soon as possible. While these reactions are likely to be broadly similar for young people of any ethnicity and subject to the same experience of racism as any non-white child, for young people of mixed race these responses have been strongly influenced by the attitudes of both pupils and teachers towards their mixedness. Kathleen's comments illustrate the complexity of the mixed race school experience:

… from the first day I was treated differently from the others, by both teachers and pupils. I was the only mixed race child in my school for the first four years … Some white teachers told me that they expected me to do better than the black kids because I had white blood in me, but the black kids hated me because of it. Other teachers told me I was doomed to failure because of my heritage.

Although one of the older participants, Kathleen's experience of racism from both black and white people was shared by many younger participants who reported being confronted with racism in secondary school. This was something they had not experienced in the primary years. It is highly likely that peers did not attach meaning to difference in the primary years and therefore they did not experience prejudice in the way older children might. While it is evident from some accounts that racist insults did occur during this period, these insults seem to be neither given nor received prejudicially.

Although wanting at times to be seen as black and sometimes 'passing' as white, most participants were at the butt of racial and prejudiced taunts that set them apart as neither black nor white. Thomas recalls such an incident:

I remember an altercation with a black boy in secondary school … who labelled my 'white' tone of voice and manner 'a disgrace to the black race'! As regards any schism between my appearance and my behaviour, it has sometimes been black people, guys in particular, who find me hard to 'read' and have acted the most abruptly.

A number of people described the different 'escape routes' they used, which helped them to get through the school years. For those whose homes were less stable, like Anna, the attitudes of peers and teachers exacerbated the difficulties at home, leading to risky behaviours. Five people talked about playing the class clown. Suhail describes trying to be popular by cracking jokes in class, and Tina says that, contrary to her basic personality, she started to impersonate people and do things like that to make people laugh, even though she saw herself to be a very serious person.

Others coped by immersing themselves in books, music and drama. Emile, as we have seen, found refuge in hip hop music and culture as a way of distancing himself from whites who racially abused him, noting: 'I rebelled against everyone who was white … my mother, my white family, my teachers, other children at school and myself. I had severe identity crisis, didn't know who I was and where I could fit in.'

Louise turned to performance as a means of coping:

I never tried to fit in to the black scene and I used drama and acting as a way of not having to fit in anywhere … when I was very young I fitted in in the playground quite a lot but I used a lot of escapism – a lot of singing and role play.

Managing unrealistic expectations

Unrealistic expectations from both teachers and other adults, that children of mixed race would be fully conversant with both sides of their cultural heritage, were reported by many of the participants. Tracey's account shows the very mixed expectations in this area:

> One time when I was probably in first or second grade, a new student arrived who, as it turned out, was Korean. Some of my friends knew I was part 'Asian' and insisted that I try to speak some Chinese to her – they wanted to know what nationality she was since she couldn't speak any English. I told them I could only count to ten and that even if she were Chinese I'd look pretty dumb reciting numbers to her.

Suhail, whose father is a Kenyan Asian, gives another clear example of a teacher's lack of awareness or understanding of the likely nature and cultural experience of mixedness: '… it is often assumed that students from mixed backgrounds know everything about both sides of their culture. "How do they spend Christmas in India?" I wouldn't have had the faintest idea.'

Inevitably some of the experiences described are similar to those that any child might have faced. However, young people of mixed race appear to see these experiences as linked to their mixedness and different from those of other young people who, while possibly the butt of racist prejudice, are able to identify closely with others as in-groupers. These themes are also evident in the study by Tikly and others (2004) who draw attention to this lack of a 'mixed race' group in their education study. The mixed group has to deal with racism/prejudice from both black and white peers, and, in some cases, has to balance the expectations of their 'white' heritage against the stereotyping of their black or 'other' identity. These are experiences that other young people do not share.

There are varying descriptions, too, of the ways in which schools dealt with racist bullying, either as a result of parents' intervention or in its absence. Although there is some evidence of schools being seen to take the issues seriously, the overwhelming impression from the people interviewed is that very little was done to address the bullying or to put things right.

A number of people suggested ways in which things could be improved for pupils of mixed race. Aileen wants to see issues for mixed race young people taken up more widely and argued that there is a need to look at what schools actually do to raise awareness with teachers and to provide support services.

Access to groups outside the family and school

Surprisingly few of the people interviewed for the research study recall having been involved in activities outside family and school. Where they do, Guides, Brownies and Scouts are mentioned, and are seen as inclusive environments.

As well as participating in these activities several young people had enjoyed music, drama and dancing in their spare time, joining clubs and going to events. Louise did ballet and drama, Mary attended a youth club and went disco dancing, Sarah also went to a drama club and was involved in sports. Jack mentions baseball and church, and other participants mention that their siblings were churchgoers. Both Anna and Sarah talk about going to concerts and festivals.

For those young people who did access community activities the study shows that, in common with all young people, these met a real need in their lives to escape and perhaps be someone, or somewhere, else and to feel included. However, the experience of being part of the black community was an important factor for some in the search (not always successful) for an identity. Several participants describe how this was achieved.

Louise had considerable involvement with the black community when she visited her father in inner London but she stresses that her knowledge of black issues is no different to anyone else's. Like others in the study she experiences being seen as fully conversant, erroneously, with the cultures of both sides of her heritage and as a young adult she has appreciated having a mixed group of colleagues: '… a group of about four or five of us with different cultural backgrounds but mostly English – I know I found it quite helpful'.

The experience of isolation

Many experiences are proscribed by the place in which the participant grew up. Participants in the research study come from across the world, providing data to show that, while there are many commonalities of experience, where people grow up and the type of community they live within is highly significant in how they perceive, and feel about, their mixedness.

Although living in and experiencing a multicultural environment was, for many of the study participants, a positive experience, it did not necessarily mitigate their sense of difference and isolation. Some grew up in very culturally and ethnically mixed areas where they were able to move across the black/white divide and find people like themselves. Others felt much more isolated, either because they were the only person with a different skin colour or the only person with racially different parents in their neighbourhood. Many reported that neither black nor white groups included them.

As we saw in Chapter 3, there can be protectors for children of mixed race, and one of these is identified by Pinderhughes (1995) as 'geographic location – where the sense of difference is minimized'. In other words, if you grow up in a multicultural, multi-ethnic environment as a person of mixed race you do not stand out in the same way as you might in a totally white or black environment. However, Pinderhughes is careful to say that 'sense of difference is minimized' and we can see from the following accounts that, while the place where people were brought up is an important factor in how they experience their mixedness, being mixed is also experienced as difficult in the most ethnically mixed areas.

It is evident from the following accounts that while environment has a major impact, a complex system is in play that includes geography, culture and class as well as the racial mix of parents and the dominant culture of the home. Experiences are affected to some extent by the age of the participants, which ranges from 21 to 56 years (the majority being in their 20s and 30s) and thus caution is needed in the interpretation of some of the data because society has undoubtedly changed in the last 10 to 20 years. However, while many people, particularly those living largely outside London, see living in London as a much more comfortable option than living elsewhere in the UK, the sense of isolation and being the 'only one' persists. In contrast, Mary, now in her 30s, spent her childhood in a small Yorkshire town where she feels little has changed. She noted:

> Looking back now I feel that because it was small and also predominately white, I was aware of my skin colour from an early age. I remember running home from school because I had been called names … I still work in (town) and ironically enough at my old high school the children to this day don't really see lots of other cultures so the cycle continues.

A quite different circumstance is presented by Carla, also in her 30s, who suggests that although she grew up in London in a very multicultural area, her own experience was 'Western'. She says:

> I grew up in a very mixed area … where in my class it was quite a mixture of different backgrounds. It wasn't an all white area and I didn't really think of where I was from. I didn't really think of myself as anything, I was just me. I didn't really see myself as different in terms of race or anything … But we grew up in a mixed area, it wasn't real black culture with food and stuff like that. We were quite Western.

Like many other participants in the *Mixed Experiences* study, as a young adult Thomas experienced life in London and missed this when returning home to Liverpool:

> … my three years down South were an eye opener (in ways I can only now appreciate, on reflection). The wealth of opinions and experiences all brought into the capital made me grow up faster than I had before, and gave me a sense of belonging that was so much deeper, I began to take it for granted. Coming back to Liverpool (out of financial constraints) has reminded me how thrillingly anonymous I felt in London …

Sarah, now in her 20s, who went to school in a northern town, also speaks fondly of London and the general growth in the numbers of people of mixed race:

... other than my family I didn't really know anyone else who was mixed race ... but I think I really like it when I'm walking around London or pretty much wherever now and you see it (mixedness) so much more and I think that's really nice – I really like that.

The London theme recurs frequently in the *Mixed Experiences* interviews, with the participants describing the relief and joy at seeing others 'like yourself'. Theo, also in his 20s, who grew up outside the UK but is now living here, enjoys the anonymity London affords him, noting: 'in London you are basically nothing special you are anonymous you walk around as nothing special which is quite nice'.

These accounts affirm the multicultural, cosmopolitan nature of the capital, whilst indicating that racism still exists under the surface. Those participants who grew up outside the UK had other experiences. Theo was first-generation mixed in Cayman, and was unusual in a country where most people are multi-generationally mixed. He describes Cayman as:

... a place where there are a lot of mixed people multi-generationally not first generation ... so I wasn't anything special ... I certainly was different, it wasn't such a big deal I suppose. I wouldn't say I was teased or something like that but it was recognised that I was first generation.

In *Mixed Experiences*, those people growing up as mixed race in other parts of the UK appear to have experienced more racism and isolation, but this is not a consistent finding as their lives are affected by class and family cohesion. Other factors such as broken families, single parenthood and time spent in public care are unrelated to geographical location, although it is possible that the geographical isolation some respondents describe could have been a contributing factor to family vulnerability.

Most of the participants growing up as mixed race outside the UK have experienced living in more than one country. They describe being seen as black in some places and white in others. Theo and Kelly were both brought up in places where being mixed was the norm and only experienced being seen as different on going to other countries for their higher education. The accounts of these participants act as an important indicator of the way that ethnicity and skin colour play differently in different societies – that is, the social construction of race.

Summary

A strong message emerging from the experiences people describe in this chapter is that children and young people of mixed race need to be acknowledged as such, provided with good role models (possibly through the school curriculum) and afforded the opportunity to talk with others of mixed race if they feel the need. The situation they describe is one where there is a great deal of scope for them to interpret any negative experiences as being because of their mixedness, with the consequent damage to self-esteem and threat to mental health. This interpretation of negative experiences is one that practitioners need to consider carefully.

School difficulties appear mainly in the secondary school years, and it is evident from other studies that there are very few services that offer mixed race children and young people any special in-school support.

In terms of the experience of feeling isolated within their local community, the narratives of the study participants indicate that although environment has a major impact, a complex set of systems is in play. London and large multicultural, ethnically diverse cities bring attractions and possibly a greater sense of not being 'different', but this does not prevent children and young people of mixed race experiencing racism and other difficulties in how others perceive them.

7 Risk factors for mental well-being and mixedness

In Chapter 4 the concepts of risk and resilience as they are used in the child and adolescent mental health (CAMH) field were presented. The interplay of risk and resilience was explained, as was the idea of risk and resilience being on a continuum for many of us as we grow and mature. This chapter explores the research narratives to identify whether there are any additional risks to mental health that are significant only for this group, as well as showing how resilience is developing possibly specifically as a consequence of mixedness.

Key points to note include:

- There may be risks to mental health for mixed race children and young people that are additional to those faced by all children.
- There is a range of interrelated circumstances that impact on mental health.
- Many potential risks to mental health diminish with maturity.

The *Mixed Experiences* research project was emphatically not a diagnostic exercise. Participants were not asked about their mental health, nor were they recruited on the basis of having, or having had, a mental disorder of any sort. There was no intention to pathologise or diagnose, but rather to look at the childhood experiences of being mixed race and observe the ways in which those experiences may have posed risks to mental health as well as the ways in which they may have contributed towards the development of resilience.

The narratives show that almost all participants had experiences in their childhoods that put them at increased risk of mental health problems, although none was of a sufficient magnitude to actually cause mental disorder. But if other factors, not specifically touched on by this project, such as death of a parent or a traumatic experience in a war-torn country, were also being experienced then the additional factors identified in the data would be of concern in at least one-third of the participants.

Equally, features are evident in the lives of the research participants that could be seen as factors that may have developed resilience and, in many cases, there is a clear continuum from risk to resilience.

The aggregated experiences raise concerns in a number of areas related to mental health/well-being and these are as follows:

- poor self-esteem and identity confusion
- hostile and rejecting relationships
- the experience of discrimination.

Poor self-esteem

Self-esteem is in many ways an imprecise concept. As it is used here it relates to the confidence, or lack of it, of the young person and their feelings of worth. Self-esteem can be thought of as feeling good about oneself, having a positive attitude to life and a sense of control and satisfaction about the challenges life presents. It is comparable with general happiness as described by Layard (2005) and also with general well-being.

Where children or young people lack the appropriate level of self-esteem then they are likely to feel less happy and less generally confident about life's prospects. For the participants in this project, this is evidenced in their confusion about identity and their negative views of self and personal appearance as well as the apparent/perceived lack of a clearly identifiable peer group to provide a cultural identity. In the *Mixed Experiences* sample, identity confusion is recorded by the majority of the participants.

Hostile and rejecting relationships

The experiences described in Chapter 5 demonstrate that the specific support provided by families in relation to being mixed race varied widely. Stable families, which are affirmative of their children's mixedness, help to ensure that children are able to deal with the prejudices they meet and allow them to feel comfortable in their own skins, being proud of their mixedness and who they are. In other families life experiences have been more difficult and support has not been there in a way that the child could receive it. There has sometimes been a lack of acknowledgement of any difficulties that the child has encountered in relation to being mixed race.

Poor family relationships are shown to be highly significant for the research participants, frequently arising from the fact of being mixed, in terms of rejection or hostility from the wider family; the individual's own rejection of one parent; and rejection between siblings. Where this occurs, it further emphasises the lack of belonging.

There are other descriptions of rejection that are described in the data – for example, the experiences of Tina and Anna who lost their fathers to death and divorce, and others, like that of Thomas who never knew his father, which will be shared by many children generally. However, while there is little reporting (although there is some) of hostilities between the child and one or both of the parents, there is significant reporting of hostility and, in some cases outright rejection, from grandparents and parents' siblings that is experienced as being directly related to the parents' mixed marriage.

Of the seven people with the highest intensity of risk, all but one (who passed as white) experienced isolation as a result of their mixedness and their membership of a 'mixed' family. For some this was a combination of factors, which were also about circumstances such as the separation of their parents or the stigma attached to being brought up in a single parent family, or where the marriage/partnership had been acrimonious and sometimes violent.

This raises many questions about the nature of 'mixed' relationships, and whether in themselves they are difficult and liable to attract more problems than families with parents of the same race. As has been mentioned previously, Alibhai-Brown (2001) suggests that mixed families can be much stronger because they have to be able to manage the potential disapproval of their union from family and friends, but the data from this research show that partnerships can be seriously threatened if the outside world or the wider family is unaccepting of the union.

Discrimination

For almost all participants, secondary school education in particular brought heightened experiences of discrimination and racism, from both peers and adults. Where families were affirmative and prepared to face these occurrences with their child, helping to develop their resilience, the insults and injuries are not reported as having had a serious or lasting effect. Where there has not been adequate family support the data show that participants were dealing with the resulting trauma into adulthood. These people report that they would have appreciated a fuller discussion with, and openness from, parents. But, as has been noted earlier, some families were clearly trying to be supportive to their children and found it difficult to know how to do this. The fact that the parents were mostly not themselves mixed race has meant that the immediacy of their children's experiences could not be fully shared, however positive the parents' intentions were.

The prejudice and discrimination experienced by children from their peers and others in the wider community, mainly in school but also experienced elsewhere, sometimes tempered by class and geography, is another well-documented risk factor; for example, works by Ali (2003) and by Tizard and Phoenix (2002) both refer to this issue.

The individual stories show that, as young people, the participants were on the receiving end of prejudicial and racist abuse, verbal and physical, from both black and white groups. Experience of racism is the most consistently reported factor. It is recorded by all but three participants, two of whom, Jack and Theo, grew up outside the UK in communities that were very racially mixed, and the third, Clare, grew up as white. This was their childhood perspective but it is clear that, as young adults moving in different circles, racism in whatever way it is experienced and defined by the individuals concerned has been felt to be encountered.

The geographical location in which people grew up is a factor for all participants, with many saying that growing up in London or a large conurbation is easier than growing up in a rural area or small town. This view was sometimes based on a single experience of visiting London as a young person and feeling much more integrated in that setting, seeing people like themselves and being altogether more anonymous. However, racism is still experienced in these 'easier' urban settings as are feelings of isolation from the surrounding community.

Aggregating the risks

The specific emphasis of these risks, within those that might be more generally experienced by all children and young people, should alert the practitioner to issues that may arise that are related to mixedness.

The absence of emotional damage from risk in these areas suggests that the child or young person has developed, or is in a supportive environment conducive to the development of, resiliences that could be built on and enhanced.

Table 7.1 provides a synopsis of the main risk factors considered in Chapter 4 and identified in the CAMHS literature (Health Advisory Service 1995), highlighting the risk-specific factors to emerge from this research for mixed race children. These are set out separately in the last two rows of the table, reminding the practitioner of the more nuanced approach to assessing risk and resilience that must be undertaken in relation to this group.

Table 7.1: Risk indicators and the specific risks for mixed race young people

Domains	Child	Family	Community
Potential risks to mental health for all children (Health Advisory Service 1995)	– Genetic influences – Low IQ and learning disability – Specific development delay – Communication difficulty – Difficult temperament – Physical illness, especially if chronic and/or neurological – Academic failure – Low self-esteem	– Overt parental conflict – Family breakdown – Inconsistent or unclear discipline – Hostile and rejecting relationships – Failure to adapt to child's changing developmental needs – Abuse – physical, sexual and/or emotional – Parental psychiatric illness – Parental criminality, alcoholism and personality disorder – Death and loss – including loss of friendships	– Socio-economic disadvantage – Homelessness – Disaster – Discrimination – Other significant life events

Domains	Child	Family	Community
Potential specific risks to mental health for children of mixed race (from Health Advisory Service list)	**Low self-esteem**	**Hostile and rejecting relationships**	**Discrimination**
Specific risk indicators for children of mixed race suggested by the data from this research	**Identity confusion and appearance**	**Negative and unsupportive relationships, for example denial of any issues related to mixedness by close family members**	**Isolation and experience of racism from both white and black ethnic groups**

The picture is varied, but while family attitudes and support emerge as being clear indicators of protection against risk (by aiding the development of resilience in the young person) there are other factors that strongly suggest risk, the most frequently reported of which are prejudice and racism from both black and white peers. What also emerges as significant is isolation and poor self-esteem, as a result of feeling and knowing oneself to be different and experiencing this negatively.

Although many participants reported feeling comfortable and pleased about their mixedness as adults, their childhood experiences are reported as very different. Most describe a trajectory that begins relatively positively in early childhood, becomes difficult and isolating in the teenage years but resolves positively in adulthood as resilience develops. In a very few cases the narratives do not suggest a positive resolution and there appear to be ongoing issues related to self-esteem. These less than optimal outcomes relate to other factors as well, but overall, the stories show that mixedness is a significant factor in the minds of the participants.

Resilience

The way in which attributes that promote resilience are defined in the literature shows that essentially they are the antitheses of the risk factors, and again the narratives of the *Mixed Experiences* study indicate their importance. However, resiliences can operate in some circumstances and not in others and, because they are experience-dependent, develop as the young person develops. Secure attachment is the bedrock for the development of resilience, together with consistent parenting and unconditional support for the child into adulthood. Where these are present, children and young people are able to manage significant difficulties and grow emotionally in the process. The inoculation theory, as described by Rutter (2007), provides a theoretical framework for understanding this trajectory. One would therefore expect to find that those children whose family experiences have been positive will be able to manage risks to their mental health with family support and that their resilience will build accordingly.

The stories of two of the participants, Sarah and Kelly, are examples of this, showing that although they experienced racism as children and young people, the support from their families was always strong and helped them to get through these episodes by being consistently affirming of their mixedness. Jack and Theo grew up in societies where there was no pressure to justify their ethnic/racial origins. When Jack, as a young man, comes to embrace his mixedness, he is able to do so from a position of confidence. Theo first experiences racism as a young man when he comes to the UK. However, he hardly defines it as racism and appears more amused than angry at the labels people place on him. Yet it is significant that he specifically mentions that he enjoys the anonymity of London and seeing others of mixed race around him, suggesting that he might be more unsettled by racism towards him than he openly admits.

For almost all of the other participants their difficulties as children and young people in being mixed race apparently resolve themselves in adulthood. A number of factors could be at play here including personal and professional achievements, positive adult relationships and, essentially, maturity. While two participants are clear that they would not recommend inter-racial marriage, others are pleased with their difference and experience it positively as adults, enjoying the ability to know and share in more than one culture. In a small number of instances, particularly in the accounts given by Thomas, Anna and Louise, there is an acknowledged need for more emotional stability, but this is accompanied by very positive feelings about identity.

Although many issues are resolved, with positive identity and self-esteem achieved by most participants, there remain concerns about some. It is impossible to know from this study what the longer-term outcomes might be. However, it is very clear that, during childhood and adolescence, young people of mixed race experience real difficulties which, although apparently resolved for many, are likely to be embedded in their minds. Rutter (2007) argues that this has the potential to negatively influence adult relationships and subsequent parenting if further risks to mental health are experienced later in life. The presence of resilience-promoting factors in each individual's life is crucial in this trajectory.

Inconsistencies of experiences

The narratives provide evidence of the development of resilience and demonstrate again that risk and resilience exist on a continuum. However, a significant proportion of participants experience behaviours that damage their self-esteem from the same individuals whom they credit for helping to develop their resilience.

The research identifies a range of family environments, from those families that are dysfunctional much of the time and offer very little affirmation of mixedness, through those families who demonstrate both affirming and rejecting behaviours, to those who are always positive and nurturing (at least in the experience of the participant) towards the mixedness of their children. This experience of parental support, or lack of it, and its effect on well-being is common to all children as they grow up. However, for children of mixed race, it is the affirmation or otherwise of their (racial/ethnic) mixedness by their parents that is shown to be highly significant.

This duality is apparent in many of the narratives. School and community experiences both support and undermine the mixed race young person. School friends were described as becoming cliquey and rejecting in early adolescence, after positive childhood experiences with the same young people. The differences melt away again in later adolescence for some participants who make more 'mature' relationships with their peers.

The participants' accounts do not suggest very much current negativity at all about being mixed race, which is in some contrast to earlier research writings that give more pessimistic accounts (Alibhai-Brown 2001). The increasing size and visibility of the mixed race population and, in particular, the high visibility of mixed race people in the entertainment industry, the creative arts, politics and sport could be playing a part, as some participants have noted.

This is not to suggest that there are no negative current experiences reflected in the data. Several respondents describe felt, current, overt and covert racist incidents suffered by themselves or their own children. Others mention that parents or siblings have had periods of mental illness, which they subjectively attribute to the hostile environments they experienced because they were living in a mixed race family.

Summary

This chapter has looked at the presence of risk and resilience factors in the young lives of the research participants. It has identified additional, or more nuanced, risk factors for children and young people of mixed race such as racism from both black and white people, isolation, identity confusion and rejection of one side of their heritage. These are factors that service providers across health, social care, youth justice and education need to consider in the context of risk assessment, as well as looking at ways of minimising the potential damage these risks might engender by promoting resilience wherever possible.

The chapter draws attention to the possible aggregation of risk factors for mixed race young people in some very specific circumstances, where additional risks were present, that would give rise to enhanced concern about poor mental health outcomes. It identifies those circumstances that foster and develop resilience such as positive family relationships and positive endorsement of mixedness. It shows that even when difficulties do arise that are related to mixedness, there are circumstances in which resilience can develop as a direct result, exemplifying the inoculation, or steeling, process described by Rutter (2007).

8 Services for children and young people of mixed race

A number of the studies cited have concluded that more needs to be done to improve service delivery and sensitivity to children of mixed race; for example, Ali (2003), Alibhai-Brown (2001), Patel (2009) and Williams (2011). Although there are some projects that do address these special needs, written accounts of them are few – a finding reconfirmed by the *Mixed Experiences* study when searching for models of good practice in supporting children and young people of mixed race.

Key points to note include:

- Poor access to services for people from minority ethnic groups is longstanding and it is quite likely that children and young people of mixed race are equally affected (given the issues of the misclassification of mixed race often found in national data sets concerning ethnicity).
- In the mental health field the difficulties of access to CAMHS for BME children and young people have been well documented (Malek and Joughin 2004; Street and others 2005; Malek 2011). On the other hand, young people from minority ethnic groups are disproportionately represented in a number of areas of public service provision (see Chapter 2), which may be indicative of a failure of services elsewhere to intervene early to address their needs and prevent an escalation of their difficulties.
- A small amount of literature exists that has considered the ways in which treatment and support can be most effectively given to BME young people and their families (Dogra and others 2002; Sinclair and Hai 2003) and this is likely to have some relevance to children and young people of mixed race. Much of this work cautions against 'colour blindness' and institutionally racist behaviours (Walker 2003; Maitre 2002).

Elements of good practice in working with different ethnic groups

Despite the paucity of literature about services specific to children and young people of mixed race, some of the learning and core principles as to what works in supporting children and young people from different ethnic groups may provide useful pointers for practitioners.

In the *Minority Voices* guide to good practice (Kurtz and others 2005), the following are identified at various stages in the provision of services:

- In terms of the strategic planning and commissioning of services, there should be careful and expert assessment of the needs of BME young people, carried out jointly with local BME communities; identified needs should also be addressed in a non-stigmatising manner.
- Involving voluntary sector providers, and working with BME organisations and young people in such a way as to actively engage them in the process, is a key part of raising awareness and in ensuring that services are accessible, acceptable, flexible and well-matched to the needs of the relevant population group.
- There needs to be widespread cultural awareness among staff and respectful working with local groups and agencies, with staff from those same communities wherever possible. They should be operating in an environment that shows understanding and sensitivity to diverse cultures. Receiving help from staff who are interested and aware of cultural differences and who do not make assumptions about a young person's situation, is especially useful.
- Good practice includes careful monitoring of access to, and of the outcomes of, provision by BME and other groups of young people in order to ensure that no groups are either under-represented or disproportionately over-represented, drawing on local population data.

Examples of projects focused on supporting mixed race young people and families

Internet and telephone inquiries, undertaken at the end of the *Mixed Experiences* study, generated very limited material about services.[3] In a number of cases it also appears that in the past five years some services have lost their funding and have closed.

There are clearly common features of the following services, in that they provide opportunities for people of mixed race to meet together, to share

---

3 Other available resources are often buried in other material. For example, the Pre School Learning alliance website has some helpful content and offers to provide training for pre-school staff on mixed race. https://www.pre-school.org.uk/providers/inclusion/544/how-can-we-support-the-identities-of-our-mixed-heritage-children

experiences, explore issues of racial identity and to offer advice and support to one another.

The Mosaic project

Based in Brighton, Mosaic exists to empower black, Asian and mixed parentage families to combat racism and to support the development of positive cultural and racial identity. With a team of four staff, Mosaic aims to create safe, supportive and culturally diverse environments for people and families of black, Asian and mixed parentage backgrounds, and to provide opportunities for them to positively explore their cultural and racial identity.

Mosaic currently has an approximate membership of 2,461 members who are all from black, Asian and mixed parentage heritage. Of these, 1,147 are adults and 1,314 are children and young people. Approximately 68 per cent of the children and young people seen at Mosaic are of mixed parentage. Some 84 per cent of adults are non-white, which includes 20 per cent who are of mixed parentage: 18 per cent are African, 11 per cent are African-Caribbean and 10 per cent are Asian.

The Mosaic team provides advice and information on issues related to race and cultural identity and run the following activities:

- social gatherings and outings
- a monthly drop-in
- an under 5s playgroup
- a telephone helpline
- a library and resource room.

The project also publishes a newsletter; inputs into local policy forums to represent the interests of people and families of black, Asian and mixed parentage backgrounds; runs advocacy training; supports a youth forum; and provides volunteering opportunities for local people. (Further information is available from the project's website – http://www.mosaicbrighton.org.uk – or by emailing Mosaic on info@mosaicbrighton.org.uk)

People in Harmony

People in Harmony (PiH) is an organisation established in 1972 to promote the positive experience of interracial life in Britain and to challenge the racism, prejudice and ignorance that exists in society.

Its members include people of different ethnic and cultural groups, mixed race people, families and couples and adoptive and foster families. Members work together to ensure that all children can grow up in a society in which they feel they belong. Children are encouraged towards creative self-definition and self-expression through photography, literature, music and poetry.

Via mutual support, largely through an established website and seminars, members create opportunities to explore mixed race issues and to challenge racism. Membership is nationwide and PiH is keen to recruit members and volunteers, to set up local support groups and develop a network of contacts with experience relevant to its aims.

Its activities include:

- advice, support and information
- a telephone helpline and support to a network of local groups
- annual conferences in London
- a regular newsletter and other information resources.

For further information see the PiH website (http://www.pih.org.uk/), email info@pih.org.uk or telephone 0845 468 0755.

The Multiple Heritage Project Mix-d:

The Multiple Heritage Project, which is now known as Mix-d: was established in 2006 to work with young people of mixed race in and out of school settings to develop their self-esteem and a positive mixed identity. Its mission has been to:

- remove the awkward silence surrounding the subject and resolve an unsettled political topic
- encourage young people to engage constructively with their identities
- equip professionals with the understanding, terminology and experience to interact confidently with the subject
- develop carers'/parents' knowledge in all aspects of developing positive racial literacy for their child
- share this expertise as widely as possibly through speaking, teaching, listening and developing materials.

These aims have been achieved through a range of activities, including work with young people of mixed race in schools and colleges across the UK; conferences around the UK for young people of mixed race, both regional and national; events such as modelling contests and the development of a 'Mix-d Museum'. Mix-d: has also produced a parenting guide and a pack for professionals to enable people to work confidently around mixed race issues.

For further information, as well as access to the resource packs, see the Mix-d: website (http://www.mix-d.org/).

Intermix

The Intermix website (http://www.intermix.org.uk) started in 1999 for the benefit of mixed race families, individuals and anyone who feels they have a multiracial identity.

Its purpose is to offer friendship, support, information and advice to mixed race individuals, their families and carers, racially mixed couples and transracial adoptees.

Intermix also aims to:

- explore the mixed race experience and the concept of racial identity by bringing mixed race individuals together, to ensure that they, their

    families and society at large have access to balanced and sensitive
    portrayals of racial duality
- highlight the marginalisation and racism faced by mixed race
  individuals and racially mixed families living in the UK
- help mixed race individuals explore all of their heritage
- promote a positive attitude between and towards mixed race
  individuals, their families, racially mixed couples and transracial
  adoptees
- highlight the achievements of mixed race individuals in society.

Intermix publishes a regular newsletter and runs online forums to ensure
that mixed race individuals are able to meet one another, ask questions,
voice their opinions and share experiences.

9 The challenge for practitioners

This concluding chapter draws together the main findings from the research study and revisits the key learning points and issues. From the data in a number of studies, not just *Mixed Experiences*, it is clear that young people of mixed race experience difficulties in their childhood that are, in a number of ways, quite different and often additional to those of their non-mixed race peers. Furthermore, in *Mixed Experiences,* these experiences are, or are perceived as being, centred in their mixedness.

Key points to note include:

- In the UK, the population of mixed race children and young people has grown significantly in recent years and looks set to continue to do so in the immediate future. This makes it ever more vital that public services from all sectors (health, education and social care) develop approaches to working with this section of the population in ways that are effective, that promote access and that are sensitive to needs.
- The non-heterogeneity of mixed race children and young people – their very varied experiences, social and family circumstances – requires practitioners who are sensitive in working with diverse cultures backed by personalised service approaches.
- Being a child or young person of mixed race can bring with it increased risks for mental health, but also experiences that promote resilience. Understanding the complex interplay between risk and resilience factors in a child or young person's life is an essential prerequisite of the knowledge all practitioners working with children and young people should possess.

The main issues

The research on which this book is based, plus the literature reviewed in Chapter 3, indicate that there is a wide range of issues that may need to be borne in mind when working with children and young people of mixed race.

Identity confusion

Almost all the participants describe feelings of identify confusion, which appear to resolve, at least partially, in young adulthood. They do not identify clearly with one or other parent and it is unlikely, other than perhaps in the large conurbations, that they can identify with any others in their peer group. The heterogeneity of their different identities makes this a practical impossibility. From this arises a strong need to be seen as who they are with the racial mix that they have.

In adolescence, when the search for identity is particularly important and when all young people are searching for autonomy from their parents/ carers, young people of mixed race find themselves cast adrift from their peers and placed in the role of 'outsider'. They employ various techniques to deal with this isolation, ranging from becoming the class clown to retreating into themselves or resolving to 'just get on with things'. Some find that they can pass for white and appear to become more involved with white friends. Others see themselves as black and adopt this identity stridently for a period, seeing it as a safer place to be.

As young people they may experiment with trying to be seen as black or, by default, are seen as white. In being seen as white these young people have difficulties in owning their blackness, feeling particularly uncomfortable when it seems that their friends have not recognised that they are not 'just' white or 'just' black. While striving to achieve an autonomous identity is part of the maturing process for any young person, there is an additional ingredient for these young people as they struggle to give the ethnicities of both parents the proper place in their own developing adult identity, a key part of which is their self-acceptance of their epidermal appearance.

This struggle for a comfortable identity resolves itself for most of the participants as they emerge into young adulthood and adult life, appreciating the benefits of being part of more than one culture and enjoying their uniqueness. The process of maturation is inevitably a significant factor in this transformation, and the concomitant development of resilience from the participants' varied bases is important. However, the experiences in childhood and adolescence will remain with the individual at some level.

Self-esteem and isolation

The sense of poor self-esteem is conveyed in the use of some self-deprecating language – noticeable in the way participants have expressed their views and told their stories. There was a sense that something was 'not right' with how they were, that they saw themselves as 'ugly'. These negative phrases were commonly used to explain how participants had felt as they were growing up.

Even where people talk about having friends and close family, a sense of difference and isolation was still frequently experienced. For some this is pronounced, in that their families themselves appear to have no close friends.

Secondary school experiences

Isolation is experienced most strongly at the secondary school stage where, in adolescence, peer groups form around ethnicity and culture in the adolescent search for identity confirmation, leaving those young people of mixed race on the outside. For almost all the participants this has been a difficult period, from the rejection by people who were previously their friends to the racism that they felt was in the system and emanated from teachers. While several people reported themselves as 'being difficult' at school and therefore perhaps not easy for their teachers to manage, it is quite possible that this difficult behaviour was provoked by the felt impact of systemic negativity.

Teachers have variously expected that their mixed race pupils will underachieve and have exhorted them to work harder to overcome this perceived disadvantage. In some cases children have been expected to have a level of understanding of their two or more cultures that they did not have, and there seems to have been little recognition or understanding by teachers of their pupils' domestic environments.

Racism

Like the phenomenon itself, racism has been both overt and implicit in the lives of the participants in the research study. Its appearance in school has been referred to, but it has also been felt in the home and as part of the experience of a wider isolation. Some people have described racism as being endemic in their families where one parent has seemed to demean the culture and traditions of the other. In as many as two-thirds of families it was possible to identify the dominant parent from which it is reasonable to assume (and it is sometimes expressly evidenced in the data) that the culture of one parent was suppressed, although possibly unintentionally.

The statistical data show that people of mixed race generally are more likely than any other group to experience racist abuse. Covert racism, such as a lack of visibility of mixed race people in teaching materials, was also identified. Several participants mention that this issue of invisibility is an area where changes need to be made for the future.

Family support

The data provide a great deal of evidence to demonstrate the importance of family for all participants. Many indicate that, in their view, their families did not do enough in terms of supporting their mixedness, expecting them to fit in, to achieve unreasonably, being unaware of what they were experiencing and being unable to say anything that was helpful to deal with their personal anguish. Some parents are reported as being racist themselves, albeit unintentionally, and there is significant reporting of hostility from grandparents on one or both sides of the marriage. Sometimes this is short-lived but often it lasts for the lifetime of those grandparents.

Where families have been positive about their child's mixedness, the experience of being mixed is positive, establishing the child's identity appropriately and building their resilience and self-esteem. There is no indication in the data that the main parent was ever consistently negative towards or about their child.

In these families, as in any group of families, there have been examples of a lack of consistent parenting and an increased instability generally. Both of these factors undermine mental health and have been difficult for the participants to cope with, as they would be for any child. However, in these cases a significant link to their mixedness was made by the participants, suggesting that the mixed relationship per se put extra strain on the family. This is a complex phenomenon that practitioners need to be aware of.

Significant family members

Several people describe strong mothers, both black and white, and strong and nurturing grandparents. These attributes are not spoken of in relation to fathers, although Thomas talks very positively of his grandfather's influence, confirming the importance of mothers generally in the transmission of culture and nurture.

The data on siblings are interesting in showing that the experiences of brothers and sisters who are living in the same family can sometimes be quite different. Skin colour and being in different geographical locations at different ages can have a large effect on why siblings' experiences differ. Where siblings have been able to pass as white, their friendship groups differ from sisters and brothers who are visibly mixed race or seen as black.

In all these varied family situations there is a tension around being mixed. Even where parental support is shown to be strong, the data indicate that children were aware of the inherent difficulties, or the existence of issues that others did not experience. In cases where family support has been strong, children's resilience has been developed in ways that have helped them to establish their identity and to deal with racism. Where family support has been intermittent or weak, as well as more or less non-existent, participants have not spoken with much confidence about their ability to manage racist incidents or to feel good about themselves and positive about their mixed status.

Geography and socio-economic factors

Geographical location is an important factor for young people of mixed race, with the inner city providing an easier environment than outer suburbs or country districts. London is most frequently cited as the easiest place to be, though growing up in outer London is not experienced as being as easy.

Unsurprisingly, socio-economic status is shown to be of significant importance. Some participants who grew up in the inner city cite other factors as being isolating, such as being in a single parent family and spending some time in care. But socio-economic factors, which affect mono-racial children too, are also a significant mediating factor in how children of mixed race negotiate their childhoods.

Risks to mental health

The picture is varied, but while family attitudes and support emerge as being clear indicators of protection against risk (by aiding the development of resilience in the young person) there are other factors that strongly suggest risk, the most highly reported of which is racism. As we have seen, what also emerges as significant are isolation and poor self-esteem, as a result of feeling and knowing oneself to be different and seeing this negatively.

Most people describe a trajectory that begins relatively positively in early childhood, becomes difficult and isolating in the teenage years, but resolves positively in adulthood as resilience develops.

The increasing size and visibility of the mixed race population and, in particular, the high visibility of mixed race people in the entertainment industry, the creative arts and sport could be playing a part in the development of more positive feelings, as some participants have suggested. It is also very evident that the election of Barack Obama as US president in 2008 has had a profound, positive effect.

Future implications

The demographic evidence of the young, fast growing, mixed population indicates that greater recognition of this group is warranted, both in research effort and service delivery, which implies policy development. Data from the 2011 Census provide more opportunities for understanding trends in the mixed population. Identifying people of mixed race as black, effectively following the US 'one drop rule', or in other cases choosing to do this as a political and social statement, is no longer acceptable to many mixed race people.

There has been a growing popular discourse on mixed race, partly as a result of the Obama campaign and subsequent election in 2008 and also prompted by sports and media stars and politicians being explicit about their racial heritage – for example, Tiger Woods, Ryan Giggs, Oona King and Jessica Ennis-Hill. In spite of this the acceptance of mixed race as an identity is still far from universal and 'black' is frequently the default position in popular discourse. This makes no sense for those people of mixed race who identify as mixed and even less sense to those people who identify as white. Although people of mixed race have on the whole found it easier than black people to mix with white people – in extreme cases being used to 'go between' the two racial groups, as in the slave trade – this has not been on the basis of full acceptance or equality.

The discourse on mixed race has from time to time been preoccupied with the idea that mixed race people are in some sense the embodiment of a solution to problems of racial/ethnic disharmony. This position is not shared by many people of mixed origins, and while it cannot be concluded that children of mixed race are the future, in terms of equality and racial harmony, they constitute a growing demographic category and are likely to be increasingly vocal about the positive and negative aspects of the multiple heritages each enjoys.

While public health, social care and education policies and practices are developing to meet the mental health needs of all children, it is essential that the specific issues that are important to children of mixed race are considered and included if this growing population is not to continue to feel isolated and undervalued. This can only be done effectively where these specific issues are understood and where practice is modified and enhanced to ensure optimal mental health for every child and young person of mixed race.

A number of recommendations for service changes were articulated by the research participants, most of which focus on training practitioners in the field to be aware of the concerns of mixed race children and young people. Other recommendations centre around the provision of role models in schools, showing the place of people of mixed race in history and highlighting current achievements by people of mixed race. Some suggest that support needs to be available in schools to students of mixed race.

Aileen, for example, would like to see more pressure put on service agencies generally to make provision for children of mixed race, and reiterates again the need for further research:

> The government needs to put pressure to make sure that the public services are equipped and knowledgeable … I think that organisations dealing with young people from a mixed race background, and adults, need more support, more capacity building and more guidance for the services they should be providing. I think that's an important move that the government should make to try to increase the body of research that's out there.

From the data presented in Chapter 2 it is evident that children and young people of mixed race are disproportionately over-represented in a number of categories of vulnerability. In order to address this, more needs to be understood about the mixed race population as to why this should be.

Summary

In summary, while children of mixed race deal with many of the issues that all children face in growing up, there are also additional and different issues around identity, isolation, family support and racism that need to be understood by practitioners in the field who are making needs assessments of mixed race children.

It is not good enough to use 'black' as a default description for people of mixed race. The evidence from the *Mixed Experiences* research project is clear that young people of mixed race wish to be seen as who they are, with their individual ethnic mix. Policy and practice must reflect this.

Parents of children and young people of mixed race will, in some cases, need and appreciate specific backing to enable them to support their children appropriately, to deal with racist bullying and with issues that their children bring to them.

All practitioners working with children of two or multiple ethnicities/ heritages need to be trained to have an appreciation of the difficulties that this group might experience. Help with the development of resilience and the minimisation of risk to the mental health of the young people for whom they become responsible in whatever setting must form part of this training.

Ideally, projects to support mixed race children and young people need to be developed across the country, given the small number of projects that currently exist in the UK. Until there is universal support, opportunities can be created to learn from existing projects and to replicate their learning where possible.

The need to reduce the vulnerability of mixed race children and young people, thereby reducing their disproportionate presence in the indices of vulnerability, goes without saying. A better understanding of the very specific experiences of these young people is essential if this is to be achieved.

In working with children and young people of mixed race, practitioners must:

- allow them to choose their own identity, resisting any pressure to pigeon-hole them
- understand the potential for identity confusion in adolescence
- appreciate that moving to secondary school may have additional difficulties for this group
- realise that the approach of families is all important for these young people, and that families will vary greatly in the way they manage
- give due weight to the factors that may be isolating the family and the young person
- never make assumptions about family culture, practices and relationships
- make opportunities to develop resilience – many tools are available
- learn from projects that do exist and, most importantly, from the young people themselves
- accept that racism is endemic and will be received by children and young people of mixed race from both black and white peers.

Appendix: Information about the study participants

Twenty-one participants were recruited through the internet and, as such, are a purposive rather than a representative sample. Mainly they grew up across the UK, with five growing up outside the UK in Europe, the USA, Papua New Guinea and the Cayman Islands. No exclusion criteria were placed on the recruitment of the sample other than their being mixed race and that of the time period of approximately six months in which the fieldwork was completed.

The area in which each person grew up is recorded as L for London; UK for places other than London; and A for abroad. F indicates a face-to-face interview; T a telephone interview; and W a written account. The accounts come from 13 women and 8 men spanning an age range of 21–56 years, the majority being in their 20s and 30s.

The data do not suggest any clear differences of experience on the basis of gender. With regard to age-related differences, the experiences of those participants who are in their mid to late 40s and 50s might be expected to be generally more difficult, given the prevailing racial discourse of the time. However, although four older people describe significant difficulties associated with their mixedness, the younger participants' accounts do not differ significantly from the older participants' accounts. In some cases the younger participants describe equally or more distressing experiences, possibly because they are closer to them in time.

Table A.1: Pseudonyms, gender, father, mother, data type and area

Name	Gender	Age	Father	Mother	Data type	Area
Tina	F	56	Guyanian	Welsh	T	UK
Theo	M	29	English	Jamaican	F	A
Anna	F	46	Indian	German	F	UK
Sarah	F	20s	Guyanian	English	F	UK
Cyrus	M	30s	English	Asian	F	L
Aileen	F	22	Nigerian	English	T	UK
Noel	M	26	Irish/English	Jamaican	W	L
Rosa	F	26	Indian/Pakistani	Finnish	W	L
Suhail	M	28	Kenyan Asian	English	W	UK
Carla	F	35	Irish	Jamaican	T	L
Emile	M	23	Mauritian	Belgian	W	A
Clare	F	40	St Vincentian	Finnish	W	UK
Thomas	M	32	Jamaican	English/Welsh/Irish	W	UK
Tracey	F	25	American	Chinese	W	A
Louise	F	24	Jamaican	English	F	L
Kelly	F	25	White Australian	Papuan	W	A
Rob	M	21	Ethiopian	English/Welsh/Irish	W	UK
Kathleen	F	45	Jamaican	Irish	W	L
Jack	M	32	Creole	French Creole	W	A
Mary	F	30s	Iranian	English	W	UK
Ayesha	F	55	Pakistani	English	W	L

References

Ahmad, W (1996) 'The trouble with culture', in Kelleher, D and Hillier, S (eds) (1996) *Researching Cultural Differences in Health*. London and New York: Routledge.

Ahmed S, Cheetham, J and Small, J (eds) (1986) *Social Work with Black Children and Their Families*. London: B.T. Batsford Ltd.

Ali, S (2003) *Mixed-race, Post-race: Gender, New Ethnicities and Cultural Practices*. Oxford and New York: Berg.

Alibhai-Brown, Y (2001) *Mixed Feelings: The Complex Lives of Mixed-race Britons*. London: The Women's Press.

Aspinall, P, Song, M and Hashem, F (2006) *Mixed Race in Britain: A Survey of the Preferences of Mixed Race People for Terminology and Classifications*. Canterbury: University of Kent.

Audit Commission (1999) *Children in Mind: Child and Adolescent Mental Health Services*. London: The Audit Commission.

Aymer, C (2010) 'Feeling "other": White maternal experiences of interracial parenting', paper presented at the Across Racialised Boundaries: Inter-disciplinary Perspectives in a Changing World seminar, Royal Holloway College, Egham.

Banks, N (2002) 'Mixed race children and families', in Dwiwedi, K N (ed) (2002) *Meeting the Needs of Ethnic Minority Children – Including Refugee and Black and Mixed Parentage Children: A Handbook for Professionals*. London and Philadelphia: Jessica Kingsley Publishers Ltd.

Barn, R and Harman, V (2005) 'A contested identity: An exploration of the competing social and political discourse concerning the identification and positioning of young people of inter-racial parentage', *British Journal of Social Work*, 36, 1309–1324.

Barrett, M and others (2006) *New Ethnicities Among British Bangladeshi and Mixed-heritage Youth*. University of Surrey. Available at: http://www.psy.surrey.ac.uk/NEBY/ (accessed 18 October 2013).

Beck, U (1992) *Risk Society: Towards a New Modernity*. London, California, New Delhi: Sage Publications Ltd.

Beck, U (2008) *World at Risk*. Cambridge and Malden USA: Polity Press.

Bhui, K (2002) 'Psycho-social and psycho-political aspects of racism', in Bhui, K (ed (2002) *Racism and Mental Health*. London: Jessica Kingsley Publishers.

Binning, K and others (2009) 'The interpretation of multiracial status and its relation to social engagement and psychological well-being', *Journal of Social Issues*, 65, 1, 35–49.

Bowlby, J (1952) *Maternal Care and Mental Health*. Geneva: World Health Organisation.

Bowlby, J (1953) *Child Care and the Growth of Love.* Harmondsworth, Baltimore and Ringwood (Australia): Penguin Books Ltd.

Bradford, B (2006) *Who Are the 'Mixed' Ethnic Group?* London: Office for National Statistics.

Bukowski, G and others (2011) *The Equality Duties and Schools: Research Report 70.* Manchester: Equality and Human Rights Commission and Ipsos MORI.

Caballero, C, Edwards, R and Puthussery, S (2008) *Parenting Mixed Children: Negotiating Difference and Belonging in Mixed Race, Ethnicity and Faith Families.* York: Joseph Rowntree Foundation.

Department for Education (2011) *Adoption Guidance.* London: Department for Education.

Department for Education and Skills (2004) *Every Child Matters.* Norwich: The Stationery Office.

Department for Education and Skills (2006a) *Care Matters: Transforming the Lives of Children and Young People In Care.* London: Department for Education and Skills.

Department for Education and Skills (2006b) *Teenage Pregnancy Next Steps: Guidance for Local Authorities and Primary Care Trusts of Effective Delivery of Local Strategies.* London: Department for Education and Skills.

Department of Health (2004a) *National Service Framework for Children, Young People and Maternity Services.* Norwich: The Stationery Office.

Department of Health (2004b) *The Mental Health and Psychological Well-being of Children and Young People.* London: Department of Health.

Department of Health (2004c) *Report on the Implementation of Standard 9 of the National Service Framework for Children, Young People and Maternity Services.* Norwich: The Stationery Office.

Department of Health (2011) *No Health Without Mental Health: A Cross Government Mental Health Outcomes Strategy For People of All Ages.* Norwich: The Stationery Office.

Dogra, N and others (2002) *A Multidisciplinary Handbook of Child and Adolescent Mental Health for Frontline Professionals.* London: Jessica Kingsley.

Erikson, E. (1977) *Childhood and Society.* London: Triad/Paladin Books.

Feilzer, M and Hood, H (2004) *Differences or Discrimination: Report on Minority Ethnic Young People in the Youth Justice System.* London: Youth Justice Board.

Fernando, S (2003) *Cultural Diversity, Mental Health and Psychiatry: The Struggle Against Racism.* East Sussex and New York: Brunner-Routledge.

Giddens, A (1991) *Modernity and Self-Identity: Self and Society in Later Modern Age.* Cambridge: Polity Press.

Goodman, R and Richards, H (1995) 'Child and adolescent psychiatric presentations of second-generation Afro-Caribbeans in Britain', *British Journal of Psychiatry,* 167, 362–369.

Harman, V (2010) 'Experiences of racism and the changing nature of white privilege among lone white mothers of mixed-parentage children in the UK', *Ethnic and Racial Studies,* 33(2), 176–194.

Health Advisory Service (1995) *Together We Stand – Child and Adolescent Mental Health Services: A Thematic Review*. London: Department of Health.

Hillier, S and Kelleher, D (1996) 'Considering culture, ethnicity and the politics of health', in Kelleher, D and Hillier, S (eds) (1996) *Researching Cultural Differences in Health*. London and New York: Routledge.

Hirsch, D (2007) *Experiences of Poverty and Educational Disadvantage*. York: Joseph Rowntree Foundation.

Katz, I (1996) *The Construction of Racial Identity in Children of Mixed Parentage: Mixed Metaphors*. London: Jessica Kingsley Publishers.

Kintrea, K, St Clair, R and Houston, M (2011) *The Influence of Parents, Places and Poverty on Educational Attitudes and Aspirations*. York: Joseph Rowntree Foundation.

Kramer, T and Hodes, M (2003) 'The mental health of British Afro-Caribbean children and adolescents', in Ndegwa, D and Olajide D (eds) *Main Issues in Mental Health and Race*. Aldershot: Ashgate Publishing Limited.

Kurtz, Z and others (2005) *Minority Voices: A Guide to Good Practice in Planning and Providing Services for the Mental Health of Black and Minority Ethnic Young People*. London: YoungMinds.

Layard, R (2005) *Happiness: Lessons From a New Science*. London: Allen Lane.

Littlewood, R and Lipsedge, M (1982) *Aliens and Alienists: Ethnic Minorities and Psychiatry*. London: Penguin.

Mahtani, M (2009) 'Same difference? Developing a critical methodological stance in critical mixed race studies', paper presented at 'Thinking about mixedness and mixing: international interdiscipliniary dialogue'. ESCR seminar, London, 26 March.

Maitre, D (2002) Choosing Identities in a Globalised World: south Asians in Britain. Gaitanisis, A and John-Baptiste, L eds. *Securing a Sense of Identity new land, new homes, new cultures*. London: Separation and Reunion Forum conference proceedings.

Malek, M (2011) *Enjoy, Achieve and Be Healthy: The Mental Health of Black and Minority Ethnic Children and Young People*. London: Afiya Trust.

Malek, M and Joughin, C (eds) (2004) *Mental Health Services for Minority Ethnic Children and Adolescents*. London: Jessica Kingsley.

Maxime, J (1986) 'Some psychological models of black self-concept', in Ahmed, S, Cheetham, J and Small, J (eds) (1986) *Social Work with Black Children and Their Families*. London: B.T. Batsford Ltd.

Mmari, K, Blum, R and Teufel-Shone, N (2010) 'What increases risk and protection for delinquent behaviours among American Indian youth?: Findings from three tribal communities', *Youth Society*, 41, 382–413.

Morgan C and others (2006) 'First episode psychosis and ethnicity: Initial findings from the AESOP study', *World Psychiatry*, 5(1), 40–46.

National Institute for Mental Health in England (2003) *Inside Outside: Improving Mental Health Services for Black and Minority Ethnic Communities in England*. London: Department of Health.

Nava, M (2007) *Visceral Cosmopolitanism: Gender, Culture and the Normalisation of Difference*. Oxford and New York: Berg.

NHS Confederation (2010) *The Equality Act 2010: Employment Implications for the NHS.* Briefing no 74. Available at: http://www.nhsemployers.org/Aboutus/Publications/Documents/The_Equality_Act_2010.pdf (accessed 18 October 2013).

Office for National Statistics (2002) *The Census in England and Wales 2001.* Norwich: The Stationery Office.

Office for National Statistics (2007) *Mental Health of Children and Young People, Great Britain.* Norwich: The Stationery Office.

Okitikpi, T (ed) (2005) *Working with Children of Mixed Parentage.* Lyme Regis: Russell House Publishing.

Okitikpi, T (2009) *Understanding Interracial Relationships.* Lyme Regis: Russell House Publishing.

Olumide, J (2002) *Raiding the Gene Pool: The Social Construction of Mixed Race.* London and Sterling VA: Pluto Press.

Owen, C and Statham, J (2009) *Disproportionality in Child Welfare.* London: Thomas Coram Research Unit, Institute of Education, for the Department for Children, Schools and Families.

Park, S and Green, C (2000) 'Is transracial adoption in the best interests of ethnic minority children? Questions concerning legal and scientific interpretations of a child's best interest', *Adoption Quarterly*, 3(4), 5–34.

Parker, D and Song, M (eds) (2001) *Rethinking Mixed Race.* London: Pluto Press.

Patel, T (2009) *Mixed Up Kids?: Race, Identity and Social Order.* Lyme Regis: Russell House Publishing.

Paulin, M (2008) 'Half-white is an insult, *The Guardian*, 13 November, 32.

Pearce, J (1993) 'Child health surveillance for psychiatric disorder: Practical guidelines', *Archives of Diseases in Childhood*, 69, 394–398.

Pinderhughes, E (1995) 'Racial identity: Asset or handicap?', in Harris, HW, Blue, HC and Griffith, EH (eds) *Racial and Ethnic Identity: Psychological Development and Creative Expression.* London: Routledge.

Rutter, M (ed) (1989) *Studies of Psychosocial Risk: The Power of Longitudinal Data.* Cambridge: Cambridge University Press.

Rutter, M (1990) 'Psychosocial resilience and protective mechanisms', in Rolfe, J and others (1990) *Risk and Protective Factors in the Development of Psychopathology.* Cambridge: Cambridge University Press.

Rutter, M (2007) 'Resilience, competence and coping', *Child Abuse and Neglect*, 31, 205–209.

Sinclair, R and Hai, N (2003) *Children of Mixed Heritage in Need in Islington.* London: National Children's Bureau.

Small, J (1988) in: Dominelli, L. *Anti-Racist Social Work.* Basingstoke and London: Macmillan Education Ltd.

Street, C and others (2005) *Minority Voices: Research Into The Accessibility and Acceptability of Mental Health Services for Black and Minority Ethnic Young People.* London: YoungMinds.

Tajfel, H and Turner, JC (1986) 'The social identity theory of intergroup behaviour', in Worchel, S and Austinn, WG (eds) *Psychology of Intergroup Relations* (pp. 7–24), Chicago, IL: Nelson-Hall.

Tikly, L and others (2004) *Understanding the Educational Needs of Mixed Heritage Pupils.* London: Department for Education and Skills.

Tizard, B and Phoenix, A (2002) *Black, White or Mixed Race? Race and Racism in the Lives of Young People of Mixed Parentage,* second edition. London and New York: Routledge.

Tulloch, S and others (2007) *The Costs, Outcomes and Satisfaction for Inpatient Child and Adolescent Psychiatric Services (COSI-CAPS): Report for the National Coordinating Centre for NHS Service Delivery and Organisation R&D (NCCSDO).* Norwich: The Stationery Office.

Vivero, V and Jenkins, S (1999) 'Existential hazards of the multi-cultural individual: Defining and understanding "cultural homelessness"', *Journal of the American Psychological Association,* 5(1), 6–26.

Walker, S (2003) *Social Work and Child and Adolescent Mental Health.* Lyme Regis: Russell House Publishing.

Wallace, SA and others (1997) *Child and Adolescent Mental Health.* Abingdon: Radcliffe Medical Press.

Williams, D, Neighbors, H and Jackson, J (2003) 'Racial/ethnic discrimination and health: Findings from community studies. *American Journal of Public Health,* 93(2), 200–208.

Williams, D (2011) *Mixed Matters.* Leicester: Matador.

Younge, G (2010) *Who Are We – and Should it Matter in the 21st Century?* New York: Viking Adult.